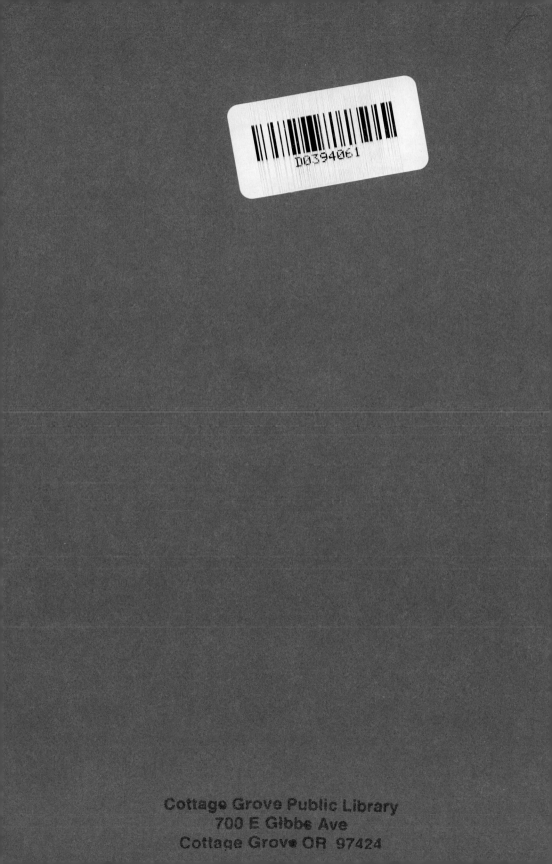

HEAVEN IS REAL, BUT SO IS HELL

HEAVEN IS REAL, BUT SO IS HELL

AN EYEWITNESS ACCOUNT OF WHAT IS TO COME

VASSULA RYDÉN

Published by alexian
an imprint of
Alexian Limited
New York • Bath

Distributed in North America by National Book Network
www.nbnbooks.com

Library of Congress Control Number: 2012955088

ISBN: 978-0-9830093-0-6

Printed in the United States of America

10 9 8 7 6 5 4 3 2 1

Designed by Bookcraft Limited, Stroud, Gloucestershire

Cover Design by Carlos Zaldivar-Five33

Table of Contents

1

Premonitions

All my life I've seen the spiritual realm. I see Angels, and Saints, and other supernatural Beings. I see the souls of dead people. I see them just as clearly as you see living people. Some people hear music in their ears and write symphonies, others see numbers in their mind's eye and solve amazing mathematical equations.

I've been called to see the supernatural …

If you met me on the street you would never suspect this. I look and act much like everyone else. I'm not a nun or a recluse or a Gypsy fortune-teller. I'm just like you, yet I'm invited to see in visions a world – a dimension – far beyond you and me.

It's an invisible world that surrounds us – a world of Angels, and demons, and powers and forces that affect every moment of our lives. I see that world, and seeing it changes the way I see our material world. It helps me grasp the hidden meaning behind so many unanswered questions in our lives.

- Where do people go when they die?
- Is there a Heaven … and a Hell and anything in between?
- Do demons or evil spirits exist, or are they just a myth?
- Does everything happen for a reason?
- If God is good, why does He allow us to suffer?
- Can dreams or premonitions tell us the future?
- Are we living in the last days?

- Will there be, in the end, any divine justice?

Unending questions … about life, and death, and what we are all doing here. The answers to many of these questions can only be discovered by seeing them from a different perspective – like turning over the backside of a tapestry to see how all the tangled threads create an elegant image.

And from my earliest days, mystical experiences were given to me by God not only to enable me to see from that perspective but for His own reasons as well.

This is a story of amazing, incredible experiences and encounters with the Divine – with God – and what they mean to me, to you, and to the whole world.

BEGINNINGS

I was in my late teens living in Switzerland when I first saw 'the dead'. They just appeared to me one day, sitting all around me on the floor of our family home. They all looked alike. Men and women, indistinguishable one from another, sitting so close to each other as though glued together. I knew they were real, though I had no doubt that they were dead. They were all the same shape: bald-headed, with greyish complexions, and they seemed emaciated. Their ash-colored garments were so plain as to be unnoticeable.

I had no idea who they were or why they chose to surround me, but I knew they were departed souls. From time to time, without any warning, wherever I happened to be in the house, I would see with the eyes of my soul this crowd of dead people. What impressed me was their silence and the respect they had for me.

I noticed that one of them in the centre of the group would lift himself above the others to give a sign, reminding the others to keep silent so as not to disturb me. They would sit there for hours, as though they were waiting for something to happen, or perhaps because they felt comfortable and peaceful. Strangely, their presence never bothered me nor frightened me. I never wondered why they were appearing to me, or what it meant. I was fully aware that no one else around me saw them, so I never brought it up, and never told anyone, not even my parents.

At first 'the dead' were silent, but later they began to manifest themselves in different ways, speaking and motioning to me so I would understand what they wanted. Much later – twenty years later – I understood the meaning of their presence. They no longer sat together in silence, encircling me, but appeared individually to me: either they would make their presence known to me or they would be signaling for help, especially for prayers. On many occasions, late at night or before sunrise, I would hear audibly a knock on the door, or sometimes the doorbell would ring. Upon opening I would not see anyone, but could sense a presence and knew that a soul was crying out to me for help.

Sometimes I would be lifted into their realm and find myself among them. My physical body was not actually transported, but in a mystical way my spirit would be present with the dead, and they could see me clearly. They knew I was not one of them, and that I was alive and still on earth. Some even showed their astonishment, as if to say, 'What are you doing here with us?'

It was clear that they were suffering, and their connection with me was a way to ask for help.

But it would be years before I knew how to respond ...

Seeing the dead was not my first experience with the 'other world'. I was not more than four years old when I began to have recurring nightmares in which I saw the supernatural world.

If anyone asks, 'Can a demon cause nightmares?' the answer is 'Yes, it can', but we cannot classify all our nightmares in this way. There are nightmares that come from natural or psychological causes. In time one learns to tell one from the other.

At the time, I was living in Egypt, born into a Greek family that had lived there for four generations. In my dreams I would get out of bed to walk into a dimly lit corridor. At the end of the corridor was a huge black dog with fearful red eyes, baring his teeth, ready to pounce on me and tear me to bits. Something inside me made me realize this dog was not a normal dog, but a demon.

At six years old these terrifying experiences moved from my dreams into my awake state. One night I lay awake in my bed when suddenly, by the dim light of the night lamp, I clearly saw two ugly hands, those of an old man, appearing before me, just above my throat. I froze with fear. As I stared at them they came lower and reached for my neck to strangle me. I did not want to yell lest I wake my family, so still lying down I struggled to avoid the hands, moving my head backwards until, still frozen with fear, I saw them no more. This vision distressed me so much that early the next morning I told my mother, 'Last night I saw two ugly hands reaching for my neck. I know they were evil because they intended to strangle me!'

My mother, seeing how upset I was, thought it best to convince me that the hands were not from an evil being, but rather from the Virgin Mary. But I always knew those ugly old hands could not have been the Virgin Mary's, and years later I would find out who they really belonged to.

At age ten, I had one of my first 'premonitions'. My parents had decided we would go on vacation from Egypt to Lebanon. My mother began making the travel arrangements, and sewing new clothes for the trip, as it was customary at that time to sew garments as opposed to buying them from department stores. We were all very excited at the prospect of traveling abroad by sea for the first time.

With the holiday preparations well under way, we went to visit some relatives. While the adults were talking enthusiastically about the upcoming holiday in Lebanon, we children all went to play.

Suddenly, an inexplicable fear seized me, filling my entire being with terror. I began to tremble, and burst into tears. Somehow, I knew without a doubt that death was waiting for me on the journey to Lebanon. I knew that if I went on that trip, I would not return alive.

This strange premonition was not in my imagination; I felt it was a supernatural intervention to save my life. I ran inside to my mother, crying, and she kept asking, 'What's happened to you? Did you fall? Has somebody hurt you?'

Everyone saw that I was terrified, but I couldn't speak. Finally, between sobs, I blurted out, 'If you take me over there I'll never come back alive!' I repeated this over and over again.

Everyone was shocked. Then one of my relatives, knowing full well how my mother would respond to my premonition, said, 'Well, I guess that's the end of that trip!'

He was right. My mother knew I had a connection beyond the natural world, and this premonition was enough for her to cancel the trip. No one objected, and for a while, no one mentioned holidays or Lebanon again.

I never came to know what the danger was in Lebanon, but it became clear to me that God was protecting me. He had a plan for my life, and He would preserve me for that purpose.

Some time later, I had a dream and it was so real to me, I immediately described it to my parents the next morning. 'I saw Jesus, and He was smiling at me.'

In my dream I was standing in a corridor filled with very bright light when suddenly, on the wall opposite me, I saw Jesus' Face. I was only a few meters away from Him. He was smiling and said, 'Come to Me!' Then an incomprehensible force like a current pulled me towards Him. I could not resist it, and found myself sliding towards Him. He said, 'Come to Me' three times, and each time the force dragged me closer to Him. I began to feel afraid because I could not control my feet. But finally, my face reached His, and then in an instant my face went *through* His.

After telling my dream to my parents, my father told my mother, 'Here's another of these dreams of hers. I don't know what will become of this child. Jesus is visiting her in dreams!'

My mother believed the dream was a sign indicating it was now safe to travel, but she changed our holiday destination to Cyprus. During our whole trip she wouldn't take her eyes off me, especially when we rode donkeys through the mountains. As my donkey trotted along the cliff's edge, my mother kept frantically pulling it toward the 'safe' side of the road. But stubborn as it was, the donkey got its way, and somehow both my mother and I survived!

About two years later, at twelve years old, I had another mystical dream. I was getting married. The Bridegroom was Christ. I was walking near Him and there were many people joyously waving palms, standing back to open a passage for Him to pass by. I was not allowed to see Him, although I felt Him by my side. Just after that I walked into a room where His Mother Mary greeted me with delight. Then, full of smiles, she arranged my hair and my dress, making sure I would be presentable for Her Son.

The amazing thing was that all during this early period of mystical dreams and premonitions, I was never a 'religious' person. I did, however, attend a parochial school, along with my brother and two sisters. Our headmistress was elderly and strict. If we students dared to roll up our sleeves, loosen our tie or unbutton our shirt collar, she would reprimand us. It didn't matter if we were dying in the stifling heat; the rules were the rules.

And when the rules were broken, a good beating would be administered by our beloved headmistress; I was called to her office many times to get acquainted with her rod. My embarrassment and my ego kept me silent, however, so my parents never knew of the swollen welts marking my thighs.

The missionary schoolteachers were too religious for my taste. We began every school day by reciting a Psalm and saying the Lord's Prayer in the assembly hall. I found it boring, and when some teachers added even more prayers, I considered them fanatic. We'd already talked to God, so why add more? I had no problem talking to Jesus in dreams, but these school-imposed religious practices did not agree with me.

On top of that, I was rather poor at my lessons, except for literature, dictation and art, and I preferred to use my wit to entertain my schoolmates. I had the knack of making them laugh, so I became the class clown. Some girls even asked to become my friends in order to spice up their lives!

My teachers, meanwhile, had rightly classified me as a troublemaker and a nuisance. Some wouldn't even allow me in their class, knowing my presence might lead to mayhem. In these early teen years, I had become a leader of sorts, but I felt rejected by my teachers. Still, my ego kept me from showing it, and I pretended it didn't matter.

Soon I was being blamed and punished even when the fault was not mine. One day our teacher, wearied by the disruptive class, decided to take it out on me. She slapped my cheek and shouted, 'Detention!'

I challenged her and shouted back, 'Double it!' which of course she promptly did. As the class froze in silence, they knew I had taken the punishment for all of them. They knew I didn't deserve it, but I had become an easy scapegoat.

Then something happened that no one would have predicted. Except God, who clearly has a sense of humor.

At the start of every school year, each class voted for a 'classroom captain', whose job was to sit in the teacher's chair and keep good order during the teacher's absence. At the end of the year, a big silver cup was awarded to the best and most disciplined class.

I could not believe it when the girls decided to make me their class captain. Obviously they imagined that I, one of the worst among them, would be a fun captain who would never report them to the teacher. And though I strongly objected to taking on this role, they all insisted, and I was appointed.

As soon as the teacher left the room, the class predictably went wild, chasing one another, standing up on the desks, yelling, laughing, and throwing pencils. It was worse than a zoo (as the animals there have cages); it was a jungle. I called for quiet, but my voice was drowned out. Finally I yelled at them, 'If anyone makes another move or another sound, I'll hand your names over to the teacher!'

Of course, they assumed I was bluffing, so they continued the tumult. No one even noticed as I began to write down their names, one by one.

When the teacher returned, I promptly handed her my list of reprobates. My classmates were stunned. Some gasped and started to cry, and others glared at me for betraying them. But I knew I had simply done my job – the job they themselves had given me.

I was given a responsibility, and I was going to fulfill it, even if that meant losing favor with my friends. Duty outweighed diversions.

From that day on, our class was 'converted' and actually became orderly. In the end, we even won the silver cup for good behavior! And by then, my teachers couldn't figure out what would come next from me – class clown or class president!

But what came next was something they would never have suspected, and it happened in the most unlikely manner.

One day as I was in religion class, listening to the story of Jesus' crucifixion, I was suddenly transported in a vision to the time and place where it all happened. I 'floated' away in my mind to Jerusalem, two thousand years ago, like I had traveled through a time machine. It was night and I could see the silhouette of the great walls of Jerusalem picked out by the crimson light and swirling smoke from the many fires lit by people to keep themselves warm. I could actually feel the cool evening breeze on my cheek and smell the wood smoke as it wafted upwards on the dry air. The low murmur of conversation was all around me, and the air electric with anticipation.

I knew it was a dark and terrifying hour, menacing, an hour of horror and an hour of agony that will remain eternally. Away from the town, I came to the olive grove of Gethsemane, where Jesus was praying in torment. It was after the Last Supper, and His disciples had come with Him to keep watch, but they were all asleep on the job. I could sense the fear, the betrayal of Judas and the abandonment that Jesus felt. But as He accepted His mission once again, the mission of dying on the Cross, I could see thousands of fearing demons taking flight when Love accepted to drink from the Cup that was being offered to Him by His Father.

Then my vision shifted to the following morning, and I found myself on the winding path out of Jerusalem, up towards Golgotha. Although it was daytime, the clouds were so low and dark that one would have thought the night was not over. My sandaled feet stood on dry vegetation and I could hear the tramp and clank of the soldiers as they plodded up the hill. These scenes were frighteningly real. All around me there were great crowds of people and in the vision I was just a small child. I couldn't see what was happening in front of me because of the throng of people, but I managed to squeeze myself around and between individuals, groups and families, until I was standing right by the path that Jesus took, carrying the dreadful Cross.

Time almost stood still and I could see Jesus clearly as He now drew alongside me. He was a youngish man, panting for breath, exhausted and near death. His Face and Body were bruised and bleeding, and He wore a cruel mockery of a crown, made of thorns. The crown had scratched and pierced His forehead and the blood ran down His Face, congealing in His eyebrows and down His cheeks. Despite the fact that He was suffering a great deal, His soulful eyes deeply impressed me. I knew that what was taking place was unjust.

I might have been a wilful, mischievous kid, but I wasn't insensitive to the suffering of others. In my compassion I was seized by a tremendous desire to grab hold of Jesus and lead Him quickly to safety, away from His persecutors and from the evil crowds baying for His Blood.

But before I could rescue Him, I found myself sitting in the classroom again, listening to the voice of my teacher reprimanding me for not paying attention in class. I looked around and wondered if the other kids noticed I had been 'gone'. No doubt I must have looked entirely 'out to lunch' during a vision like that.

I thought about how ironic this was. At the very moment when I seemed to be ignoring my teachers' efforts to teach me about God, I was actually reliving the biblical events mystically, in living color! How could they possibly have known?

They couldn't, because I never told a soul. I knew I could never describe what had taken place, and I knew they'd think I was crazy anyway. But my vision in Jerusalem was soon followed by other visions, and they were far too intense to be mere fancies. Nevertheless, I was powerless to explain them even to myself.

Back in the 'real' world, a new government had taken over in Egypt in 1956 – and it was not friendly towards the Western countries. Consequently, our city of Cairo came under attack. We were being bombed daily, and the war had a devastating effect on our society, especially for the children. Living in fear of warplanes day and night prevented anyone from living a normal life.

Eventually, the stress got to my mother, and she determined to move the family somewhere safe – to a place where bombs never fall. The answer became clear: Switzerland, a country that had been neutral for centuries.

Thus, in the middle of my teen years, a new adventure began. With virtually all our possessions sold, we left Egypt and went north to Alexandria where we boarded a ship and sailed to Italy.

Once there, I was enthralled. I had never seen the green pastures of Europe, and the bustling, colorful streets. As we traveled north from

Italy by train the colored fields and little towns eventually gave way to the white-capped mountains of Switzerland. It was amazing!

Our train was bound for Geneva but about an hour before it was due to arrive we pulled into the station of another Swiss city, Lausanne. We decided to get off and look around. After a short walk through the beautiful town, my siblings and I begged our parents to stay. With no reason not to, they agreed and we set up home there.

The transition was rough at first, but over the next three years, we assimilated well into Swiss culture. We worked hard at school and came to know our neighbors and our new country well.

By the time I was eighteen we had moved to nearby Pully, into a bigger flat set in peaceful surroundings, with a small garden and a veranda overlooking Lake Geneva. It was there that I had my first encounter with 'the dead', as I recounted earlier.

It was also at this age that I began to experience a social life, going out with my friends and meeting boys. Sometimes we gathered in small groups for coffee, a snack or a pizza. We also went to the movies and gathered at someone's house to dance to popular rock music. These get-togethers somehow never appealed to me because deep down I knew that most of the boys had only one thing in mind, to spend the night with the girl they had befriended. To me, that was not real love.

I would also experience a feeling of emptiness inside me, invading my soul. Because of my guarded attitude, my dates never lasted long. And then afterwards, I would feel depressed, knowing my behavior was odd. I blamed myself, and felt more and more like a misfit in this world.

But despite my mystical experiences, the 'real' world of dating, courtship, and love gradually started to overshadow the spiritual world. I tried more and more to be carefree like the other girls. I went from feeling like a 'fish out of water', to joining 'dry land' in an effort to fit in with society. For a girl of eighteen, that meant I should start looking for a husband.

While I was out with friends one day in Lausanne, I met Johan, a young Swedish man who was to fulfill that role. We decided to get married when he was in his twenties, and once married we moved to Sweden.

Though starting a family in Sweden seemed exciting, I had problems adjusting to the dark winterish climate, the Scandinavian temperament, and the language barrier. Worse yet, I had no friends. My husband's family pushed me to learn Swedish, but that forced me to venture out into the cold winter nights to attend Swedish lessons.

After two years, my husband finally finished his studies, and took a job with the United Nations Development Program, as a junior officer. In the middle of a Swedish winter he was asked to take up an appointment in Sierra Leone, and I was happy to escape into the warmth of Africa!

His job led to our traveling and living in many African countries. After Sierra Leone, we moved to Sudan, where my son Jan, our first baby, was born.

It was in this desert country that God once again spared my life. I was carrying a couple of bottles when one of them fell and broke, causing a sharp fragment to cut my left ankle. After a day or two, the wound became badly infected and swelled to the size of a golf ball, oozing pus.

I went to a doctor who disinfected the wound and assumed it would heal. Instead it became worse. I was unable to put my foot down to walk so I returned to the doctor. Afraid it might be gangrene, he put me in the hospital. There, he dug into the wound with a knife and scraped it clean. He then disinfected it and filled the hole with gauze – all without the help of any anesthetic. He said that the wound had to remain open to promote healing. His pain pills did nothing for me so he gave me a shot of morphine. I was in bed with my husband sitting beside me, and my evening meal was served.

When I started to eat, my breathing suddenly stopped for no apparent reason. I began to gasp for air, and was literally choking. In my mind I saw those ugly satanic hands which had come for my neck when I was a small child. In panic I shot up, overturning the meal tray, trying desperately to breathe. I could feel that Death was closing in on me. My husband ran out to call for help but could not find anyone. It was all happening so fast, and there seemed to be nothing either of us could do. Then, just when all seemed lost, I suddenly started to breathe again. It was as though someone had unplugged my esophagus.

The nurse finally came rushing in. Once she assessed the situation, she explained that the doctor must have given me an overdose of morphine, which my body couldn't handle.

The evil hands of death had tried again to get me. But God had other plans, even though I was not ready for them yet.

At the end of our term in Sudan, we moved with our nine-month-old son to Ethiopia for a new assignment of five years. There, my second son Fabian was born. Life was comfortable for expatriates, with many privileges. It was normal to employ servants, so I found a housekeeper, a good woman. With no housework or cooking to do, I had a lot of free time, and so I took up tennis. At first I played to keep busy, but later it became a passion – with clubs, tournaments, and championships.

When my second son Fabian was just two months old, we returned to Sweden. No sooner had we arrived than my husband had to leave for Africa again, spending many weeks there. Those were long weeks for me. I had no friends in Sweden, and I began to struggle with back problems, not to mention coping with the challenges of raising a baby and a small child on my own.

Not surprisingly, my marriage also started to hit hard times, and my husband and I were becoming very distant with one another.

Just when I felt that it was all too much for me, my husband was offered a long-term post in Mozambique. That sounded great to me, so we found ourselves packing again, ready to move.

I can imagine God was watching all these events in my life, lovingly observing my attempts to live a 'normal' life. But 'normal' life is filled with abnormalities, and when we handle them without God's help, our lives soon unravel.

Matters did not improve in Mozambique – my marriage was disintegrating, and I seemed powerless to mend it. Somehow he and I could not be everything for each other, and we weren't willing to fix it. So after many struggles, we finally came to the sad and difficult decision to separate. We agreed that for our children's sake we would remain friends after the divorce, but it was nonetheless traumatic for all of us.

It was my first big failure in life. I felt I had lost my bearings and lost my dignity. All of my dreams, and premonitions, and connections with the supernatural seemed to add up to nothing – I was just another person struggling through life. And I was doing it without God's help.

The time eventually came for my ex-husband to return to Sweden, and as my older son Jan was of school age it seemed wise for them to go together. There he could follow his schooling with his father by his side. I am sure Jan suffered from being parted from his mother and his younger brother Fabian; for me, it was the hardest period of my life. We got together as often as possible, but the brothers were separated and I deeply missed my first-born son. A family is meant to be a unit, connected and supportive. Breaking up that unit rips all of the members apart emotionally.

But somehow we survived, and life went on.

Eventually, I met another Swede, named Per Rydèn. He was a kind man, and despite the wounds I still bore from my first marriage, I felt I could trust him. I also knew it was important for my younger son Fabian to have a father at home to help raise him. I was older and more mature now, and I believed I could make marriage work a second time around. So Per and I were married.

Per's work also led us to developing countries, and we soon moved to Mozambique where I had lived once before, and then after two years we moved to Lesotho. A posting to this country was listed as a 'hardship post' although our daily life was not so bad. During our time there, we were caught up in something extraordinary.

Apartheid, in 1982, was at its height. One night we were awakened by the tremendous noise of tanks rolling by, machine guns firing and grenades exploding. It was horrific. Per shouted to us to remain flat on our beds, and not to stand up because bullets outside were flying everywhere. Our tin bungalow would have become a sieve if the bullets had come our way.

The violence eventually died down, but what was left in its wake was horrendous. The South African troops had massacred people everywhere. Even innocent women and children, pleading for their lives were mercilessly gunned down in cold blood.

The racial tensions in the country worsened and crime proliferated. Widespread poverty and hatred seized the nation, and it seemed like everywhere we looked, criminals were multiplying. It was anarchy. Burglars would come to people's homes in the night armed with rocks and hatchets. If people did not cooperate and hand over their valuables, they were attacked. All our friends were arming themselves and even Per and I decided to keep an iron rod near our bed and bought a plastic pistol that shot a liquid that would temporarily blind any intruder.

Ironically, during the daylight hours things seemed relatively normal. I still went to the club to play tennis, went shopping, and got together with friends. But at night, everyone feared going to bed, expecting the worst.

One night I awoke and could not get back to sleep. Time and again just as I was about to doze off an invisible hand would shake me, keeping me awake. At around 1:00 am, as I was half asleep, I began to hear a snapping sound, at regular intervals. In my mind, I saw a vision of a burglar's hands holding a large wire cutter, cutting through the mosquito net near the front door in order to reach the lock and open the door. I immediately became wide-awake, and I was about to jump out of bed, when I heard a crystal clear Voice, somewhere inside me, ordering me to stay in bed and wait. 'Don't get up yet,' the Voice said.

And again as I moved, it said, 'Not yet. Wait.'

I obeyed the Voice. It was powerful in its command, but kind. Not for a moment did it cross my mind to disobey. It reassured me over and over, telling me to wait, and soon I lost track of time.

Then suddenly, in an urgent tone, the Voice ordered me to get up. I obeyed and went swiftly to the back of the house to get a view of the kitchen door. I saw nothing amiss. I silently returned to our bedroom and slowly pulled the curtain back and there, *right in front of me*, a man was standing outside our house while his accomplice attempted to unlock the door to break in.

My husband and the boys were still fast asleep. (So much for chivalry!) They had not heard a thing and neither had our dog! But when

I saw the men outside the window, I yelled out at the top of my lungs, 'PER! THERE IS SOMEONE OUT THERE!'

My shouting awakened Per, but more importantly, it scared the intruder half to death. He jumped out of his skin! Then he and his friend ran off and scrambled over the fence like rabbits into our neighbor's yard.

At the time, I hadn't the faintest idea who the Voice was that guided me to scream at just the right moment when the burglar was outside my window. Nor did I realize that years later I would come to know that Voice in the distant land of Bangladesh.

But once again, God had been protecting me, and soon I would find out why …

2

Contact

Given all that we had experienced in Africa, we were happy when my husband received a new assignment in another country. This time we were headed to Asia, to the poor but beautiful country of Bangladesh.

There, my entire life would be turned upside down.

Bangladesh is one of most impoverished nations of the world. When we arrived in the capital of Dhaka, the throngs of people and the dense, frantic traffic overwhelmed me. I had never seen anything like it. There were beggars everywhere; even at the stoplights children and elderly people were knocking on our car window, begging. I remember becoming annoyed and thinking, 'Wow! They are like flies!' But immediately I heard a Voice within me saying, '*They are My children too.*' I did not pay attention to that Voice.

Everybody on the streets seemed like they were busy and in a hurry. Some were pulling carts piled high with everything imaginable. The traffic was maddening. All around us we were invaded by rickshaws and dwarfed by huge, dilapidated buses, hooting non-stop. Motorbikes were used as family transport with two or three children clinging to their parents. People crossed the roads at will, risking their lives as they dodged between the vehicles. Even lame people, some with severed limbs, were dragging themselves in the dust through the chaos. I wondered how any of them could survive. The trains too had their charm, with people crammed inside and hanging out of windows and doors like bunches of grapes, to say nothing of the freeloaders taking a free ride up on top.

It dawned on me that the Guardian Angels of this country must be the busiest Angels in the whole world trying to keep their charges alive.

Ironically, this would be the place where I would be drawn into a spiritual world.

Once I settled in to my new life in Dhaka, my lifestyle became similar to the one I had enjoyed in Africa; a constant round of receptions, bridge games and tennis tournaments. During the afternoons I either played tennis or modeled for friends who organized fashion shows. Mornings were devoted to painting, my other passion, as I had decided to prepare an art exhibition and had begun to paint canvases and sketch charcoal drawings.

November 28, 1985, began much like any other day, without any premonition of what awaited me. I was looking forward to seeing my friends that evening and went upstairs to the lounge, intending to prepare a shopping list of things I needed for our dinner party. With pencil poised and notepad ready to write my list, I suddenly sensed a presence: a presence looking at me. This was not 'the dead' I used to see in the past. This was very different from anything I had experienced before. My whole being was being filled with an unbelievable joy. Then suddenly I felt as though my right wrist was touched – clasped by an invisible presence. It produced a tingling effect in my wrist and hand, as though a low electrical current was passing through them. I didn't have time to think about what was happening, for at that instant a gentle but firm pressure lowered my hand onto the notepad in a writing position. I was totally bewildered and confused. I asked myself, 'What is this?' The 'electrical current' became stronger and the invisible presence began to lead my hand, guiding it to draw a heart. Then, in the center of the heart, it drew a rose, as though growing from the heart. And then it wrote these words that would forever change my life:

> 'I am your Guardian Angel and my name is Daniel.'

As these words were being written, a Voice within me spoke them and I heard every syllable as clearly as any audible voice. I was so shocked; I almost fell off my chair especially as the handwriting was so unlike my own. It was beautiful and majestic, and reminded me of the writing on icons. With these words being formed effortlessly and mysteriously by my Angel where I had intended to make a shopping list, my life took an unimaginable turn and was changed forever. I was dumbfounded and silent, holding my breath. I sat reading the words over and over again, trying to take them in.

It had been many years since those days when, as a teenager, I had encountered 'the dead' and seen visions. All thoughts of that mysterious 'other world' of my childhood had long since left me. So this manifestation of my Guardian Angel caught me off guard and had the effect of a brick falling on my head.

As the full implication of the words dawned on me, I was overcome with joy. I giggled, amazed that my Guardian Angel had contacted me, and overcome by great joy I threw the pencil in the air and almost flew round the house, my feet barely touching the floor, while I was repeating loudly, 'I'm the luckiest person on earth!'

The whole day I felt elated – light as a feather – excitedly waiting for Per to return from work. When he arrived, he immediately spotted my exhilaration and asked, 'So, what's up?'

'I … well … er … my Angel spoke to me!' I blurted out.

Per stared at me waiting to see what more I had to say.

'He pushed my hand to write what he was saying … I saw him … and I felt his presence, and well … he even wrote to me.'

'How? What did he say?'

'He just gave his name and drew a heart, with a rose coming out of it.'

It never crossed my mind that Per might think, 'Now my wife has finally flipped. She's really gone crackers, ready for a straitjacket.'

I recounted my story again and again while Per, as cool as a cucumber, listened calmly with just a few 'hmm's now and then. Was it his Scandinavian nature, or was he just too stunned to react? Then he told me that he had read quite a bit on the subject of mystical experiences in his student days. He assured me that what had taken place was not unique – it had happened to others as well.

When I heard that I said, 'Aha …' and realized my experience was certainly extraordinary, but not without parallel.

Strangely, I didn't make any connection between this new mystical experience and all the ones I had had in my past. I was simply focused on the events of that day, and the amazing phenomenon of meeting my very own Guardian Angel. As my entire life had so often revolved around enjoying myself, I just saw this as an amazing, one-off gift, and never expected that my Angel would come again.

But sure enough, he returned the very next day. And this time, to my great surprise, he brought a multitude of Angels of different choirs with him. I felt that the gates of Heaven were suddenly wide open because I could easily sense this great movement of Angels from above and all around me. They appeared to be excited and happy with that special air of expectation that precedes wonderful events. From their rejoicing I understood that Heaven was having a feast and they were celebrating. Then, in one voice, the Angels sang these words:

'A happy event is about to come!'

I knew that I was directly involved somehow, whatever this 'event' might be. I tried my hardest to guess what it was, but to no avail. Every time Heaven opened the Angels sang the same chorus, repeating the same words with only a few minutes of silence between each chorus. This continued throughout the day.

Then my Guardian Angel manifested again, and spoke his first words to me concerning God, saying,

'God is near you and loves you.'

I did not reply, and my Angel did not add anything. I just reasoned that it was typical of Angels to talk about God. After all, they live with Him!

I had no intention of sharing my astonishing experience with anyone outside my immediate family. I was not prepared to risk being ridiculed by my friends who knew me as a 'normal' person. Like my other mystical experiences, this little adventure would be a secret kept between me and the 'other world'.

The following day my Angel came again, but this time his attitude was different. He was very grave, and in a solemn voice he asked me to read 'The Word of God'. I pretended not to know what he meant. I asked him the meaning of it, saying to myself, 'Here it comes ...' Knowing full well that I had understood, he told me, using a severe tone of voice, that by 'The Word' he was referring to the Bible. I didn't like the way the conversation was going, and I told him, quite truthfully, that I didn't have a Bible. He said he knew very well that I didn't own a Bible, and instructed me to go and get one. Still arguing with him, I said that he was asking the impossible, because I was living in a Muslim country and the bookstores did not sell Bibles. He said,

'Go to the American School your son attends. There you will find a Bible in the library.'

Following this encounter, I debated whether to go, or simply stay home and refuse. I was not ready to commit myself. My thoughts centered on what my husband and friends might think of me if they saw me with a Bible in my hand instead of a tennis racket. I was sure they'd either make fun of me or think I'd lost my mind. I wondered where in the house I could hide a Bible so no one else would see it.

But one thing was certain: Daniel was very serious. And although the last thing in the world I wanted was to read a Bible, I figured it would be better to obey him. After all, an Angel was no doubt very powerful.

So I set off for the American School where the staff knew me. There, on a shelf in the library I saw a number of Bibles and received permission to borrow one.

At home I dutifully opened the Bible as Daniel had ordered, and found myself staring at the Psalms. I read some of them, but to my surprise the words were incomprehensible for me, as though written in a language I did not speak. Despite convincing myself I could get to grips with the verses, I understood nothing at all, not a word. It was a tormenting experience.

The Angel made it clear to me that in spite of the fact that God had given me so much throughout my life, I had completely failed to show Him any appreciation at all, and was therefore living in darkness, unable to see the Word of God and understand it.

In that moment, I felt a strange Light silently entering my soul. As that Light began to shine in the darkness of my soul, my whole being trembled, for the interior of my being was suddenly exposed in front of God and His Angels. I was given an insight into the state of my soul, which came as a shock to me. I experienced a spiritual poverty as never before, as though an immaterial Fire ripped my clothing off.

Until it happens to you, you cannot imagine what it feels like when God confronts you. The beautiful and serene path along which I had traveled with Daniel abruptly vanished and turned into a stormy, Heavenly Fire that consumed me, hurling me ever deeper into the reality of the black depths of my soul.

In that state, the worst ordeal was that I became fully, consciously aware of every wrong I had ever committed. What was happening to me was far beyond my comprehension. My Angel made me aware of my failures, of my sinfulness, while bitter remorse and indignation welled up inside me and I found myself shaking and sobbing with remorse, sorrow, and pain. In short, I saw everything I had done to contradict the holiness of God. At the same time as I was accusing and loathing myself for these sins, I felt agony in every fiber of my spirit, mind, and body. It felt as though I was descending into the mired depths of my soul while Heavenly flames roared, enveloping me on all sides, burning my passions to the root and incinerating all that hindered God's passage in my soul. Daniel in no uncertain terms let me know that the two worst offenses of all were how I had ignored God's blessings and misused the gifts He had given me.

This revelation of my soul brought me into another alarming experience. It felt just as though I was totally naked, covered with leprosy, and standing alone in disgrace and shame before the eyes of the Divine. It came in my mind how Adam and Eve must have felt after they had sinned, when God approached them in His pure Light facing them.

There I was, being reduced to naught when I was shown the desperate state of my real self. In short: my Angel had made me see my sins with the eyes of God, the way God sees them and not the way we see them. I began to feel the burden of my faults weighing me down. I was thinking, 'Am I being purged? Am I being punished?'

Then I found I was being dragged into yet another strange stage. The Angel made me realize how all these years I had been walking on treacherous marshlands and in darkness. He showed me that my soul was engulfed by danger and how I had never thought of praying and praising God. This unforeseen and unimagined process of purification lasted for almost three weeks.

Hour after hour, day after day I found myself forced to face parts of me that weren't in the least pleasant. I had to face reality; I had to face the way I truly was, and to admit that things were not as wonderful as they had seemed only a short time ago. The action of this supernatural Fire was melting my hardened heart, while at the same time shattering the crust as though with blows from a hammer.

I could not bring back the past, but through this revelation and purification, I was able to see more clearly into the hidden depths of my heart and into the reality of our nature. This awareness of our soul is called 'The Day of the Lord', and it is an experience that no one will escape. Everyone, man and woman, will go through a divine judgment, a mini-tribunal: an awareness of one's sins that will be shown either while we are still on earth, or worse still, after death.

Finally, after days of torment, the pain eventually began to subside and I started to feel somewhat 'normal' again. I had the feeling I had been purged and had been 'washed out'. I noticed that having gone through that sort of Fire, it created openness and a new sensitivity in my heart for others that were not there before. During the ordeal – for an ordeal it was – my Angel came to console me repeatedly. Although he could be very direct and quite pointed in his reprimands, he was also supportive and tender in a way that only a genuine friend can be. At one stage I even heard a Voice, which I presumed came from God Himself, saying to me:

> *'Do not take this as a penance, daughter; this was done to you out of the greatness of the love I have for you, atoning for your sins.'*

Following my ordeal, I began to understand Daniel's mission as I overheard him begging God,

'Oh God, let her follow You!'

I asked Daniel, 'Who were you praying for?'

He answered in a lamenting tone,

'I was praying for you.'

I was perplexed. Was I still so bad? And why did Daniel keep telling me to make peace with God? Annoyed, I even asked him,

'How can I make peace with God, seeing that I am not at war with God and I know that He exists?'

He simply repeated himself, saying 'Make peace with God.'

Later I would learn that our Guardian Angels pray for us all the time, pleading before God on our behalf. They pray that we will change our heart and turn to God, making 'peace' with Him after our rebellions.

During all this time I continued to lead my usual life, painting canvases for the exhibition, socializing and playing tennis, but whenever I felt my Angel calling me, I rushed to listen to what he had to say. In time, I came to rely more and more on my relationship with my Angel, giving him more time, but I certainly wasn't in the least prepared for a call from God Himself. I'd never heard that God talks to people, at least not to ordinary people, in our modern times. He might have conversed with prophets in Old Testament times, but that was history.

Daniel had tried to prepare me, to make me aware that my supernatural experiences were far from over. They had been given to me for a reason, and embodied something deeper and more dramatic that awaited me, the implications of which I could barely comprehend.

The fiery trial I had gone through had left me 'weightless'. In that state of emptiness, the things of this world no longer mattered to me. When surprises lose their flavor, when the material world diminishes in its value, when fear and anxieties are consumed and disappear, when the brilliant colorfulness of earthly elements turn dull and fade away, when the mind and soul are brought to serenity you reach a state of detachment.

Awareness of my sins and repentance had opened a wide door to the Divine order, and to complete freedom. After that fiery trial my soul was at peace; thereafter nothing would agitate or affect me any more. Inside my mind and soul was only submission and acceptance. Realistically I had just gone through 'Hell', but it was through that descent that the supernatural Fire melted my chains and shackles. Finally I had been set free! Liberated!

Then, in that state of mind, still dazed, a sweet smelling Breath suddenly blew across my face, and I heard a Voice within me saying with tenderness,

> *'I am your Father and you descend from Me … you come from Me … you belong to Me … you are Mine … You are My seed …'*

Hearing these words I was blown away. There I was, in the blink of an eye, standing on the threshold of the Uncreated Light. God's luminous Presence filled me, exploding through my entire being and uplifting my soul. The bright manifestation of God was far greater than anything I had ever experienced from Daniel. When Daniel visited me, I could see him with the eyes of my soul, and knew it was he and 'only' he. But God's Presence was invisible, even within me. I did not *see* Him, I only *felt* His undeniable Presence in my heart.

Daniel had told me I would be taught 'in the Courts of Yahweh', in those Courts where Angelic powers have access to go in and out.

I experienced an ineffable love and paternal compassion emanating from God. Yet not only this, His Ray of Light that enveloped my heart, mind and soul, was so bright and so powerful that it brought a peace that no one else could ever have given me, a peace only God can give even to the most agitated heart. And despite the power and Omnipotence of His Presence, He came to me with such simplicity, so delicately, and so paternally, that I was consumed in His Love.

I felt I knew Him. My soul recognized Him as a familiar Figure. I asked myself, 'Is *this* the Judge who is supposed to be so remote and severe and who easily condemns? Was I so misinformed about Him?' I just could not believe this was the same God I imagined in the past! And then I remembered: 'God is slow to anger, forgiving, loving, meek and gentle.' That is the true God! The feeling that I was standing before the Face of the Absolute surpasses my capacity to explain with ordinary words.

Somehow I knew in my soul that He winked at me and was amused, and at the same time delighted, perhaps because I was so bewildered and in awe.

He spoke again in my very being and the moment I heard His Voice I had no doubt that He was my Creator and Father. Every bone in me recognized Him as He said,

> *'Behold, I am your Father.'*

At that moment I realized that our real home is with God. I knew there and then without any doubt that Heaven exists and is our home! The earth? Nothing to do with earth. My mind reeled when I realized we are indeed the children of the Most High; that we descend from Sovereignty and Splendor and we belong to God, to Heaven … I felt different when I realized that we are all of Royal descent and that our Father is the King of kings – the bone of His Bone, the flesh of His Flesh!

This was the clearest vision, and the most convincing, that I have ever had in my entire life.

Still in shock, realizing that the Creator, the One, indisputable Essence and the Spark that motivated the entire universe – should talk as easily as that to me, just an ordinary person! Even now I marvel that this could happen. But in my mind, then and even now, the sheer power of experience makes it obvious that God can speak at any time and through anyone He chooses, and that's a fact.

I managed to grab pencil and paper to write down what He had said. While He was 'with' me I felt I could ask Him for help. I went over to the window, 'leading' Him there, and I pointed at the beggars and poverty outside and said, 'Look! Look at what the world has become.'

Very peacefully and as though unsurprised He said:

> *'Do you really believe I can help you?'*

'Yes, You can; You are God!'

He then asked me to pray the 'Our Father', the 'Lord's Prayer', in His Presence. I was so pleased that He had asked me to say something I actually knew, and without thinking I blurted out, 'Yes Dad!'

I don't know how this word slipped out. Was it because He was so paternal, so familiar, that I felt I knew Him? Was it because I, His creature, recognized Him in a mysterious way as the Maker and Creator, and therefore the Father of all? Whatever it was, I immediately froze in fear, awaiting God's reaction to being called 'Dad'.

He said,

> *'Do not fear, daughter, for I have taken this word "Dad" in my hand like a jewel.'*

I was so relieved at His answer that brimming with joy I rushed through the words of the 'Our Father'.

When I had finished, God lovingly told me that He was not pleased with the way I had said it, because I had prayed too quickly. I repeated the prayer, this time more slowly. God then told me that it was still not right because I was moving around as I prayed. Time and again I said the Lord's Prayer and each time God told me that it was not good and that I must start again. It went on for hours.

I began to wonder if God really wanted me to say every Lord's Prayer I had failed to pray throughout my whole life! Eventually, after many attempts at saying it properly I managed to please Him and at every sentence I uttered, God said, '*Good!*' He was finally satisfied.

At first I couldn't understand the lesson, and why I had to repeat this prayer in His Presence but eventually as the day went on, the last piece of crust that remained on my heart broke off and exposed me to His Love. I finally realized that I had to mean *every word* I uttered with love.

From there on many blessings covered me from the harmony and tranquility my soul received with the presence of God the Father. All the previous disturbances were now forgotten in the abundance and fullness of God, in which my soul received an intimate spiritual embrace.

3

The Dark Night

I was overjoyed in this revelation, and over the coming days my communications with God felt like those early days of infatuation when new lovers cannot get enough of each other. I wanted to be with Him constantly, and nothing else seemed to matter. It was bliss.

Then, without any warning, all communication with God and my Angel abruptly stopped. It was as if someone just turned off the light, and suddenly I found myself sitting in utter darkness.

Although I was still surrounded by family and friends, I had never felt so alone and miserable. The presence of God and my Angel were no longer with me. I called out to them, but they did not respond. I truly felt that He had deliberately shut Heaven and dragged me out into a desert to 'roast' in my loneliness. In fear and misery I never stopped calling my Angel, but he too had abandoned me.

Our tennis club was preparing the yearly tournaments so I participated, but my usual keenness and happiness were totally missing when I played. I thought, 'Are these God's methods? Does He approach to seduce us, then once seduced He kicks us out?'

At a later date I understood why God drags a soul to the desert. These are His words:

> *'I come to break in splinters the doors of your dungeons and with My Flame melt your chains of sin. I come to free you from your captivity and your iniquity and end up your debaucheries; I mean to save you, generation; even if I must drag you all the way to the desert and speak to you, showing*

you your aridity and how your whole body is filled up with darkness, I shall do it to save you; ah, creation! ***What will I <u>not</u> do for you …***'[1]

I tried to place recent events of my life in order, to make sense of what was happening: At first, to draw my attention and curiosity God had sent my Angel. Then He made me hear Heaven's melodies, giving me a glimpse of His Celestial Angelic Host in His Abode, and when I rejoiced in what I saw He dragged me out of the mud and without wasting time He charmed me, then without hesitation He 'roasted' me in the first spiritual Fire only to cast me out immediately with my open blisters in the desert, disappearing together with my Angel and shutting Heaven; altogether abandoning me in the terrifying silence of the desert to suffer and moan alone; ignoring my desperation, ignoring my agony and my distress.

Now from His 'hiding place' He watched and waited in silence for my wailings of surrender.

'What have I done that You shy away from me like this? Just as I was opening my heart to You, my God, You ran away and hid.' He did not reply.

I wanted to be delivered but now in this desert I was surrounded only by shadows and phantasms, lifeless things that do not satisfy the soul. I turned on every side looking for Him, and then looking for my Angel, but found neither of them.

For three weeks I wandered in this desert, between the flesh and the spirit, feeling more dead than alive.

Then, a strange thing happened. As I was experiencing this 'death' I suddenly sensed the souls of 'the dead' again, for the first time in many years. I saw their gray bodies, like shadows approaching me, creeping slowly out of a fog. In no time they had surrounded me. I realized that my spirit had been drawn into the place of 'the dead': Purgatory. The Purgatory of my separation from God had brought me to this Purgatory of the departed, where they too suffer from separation from God while they journey toward Him through a period of purification.

---

1 September 12, 1990

As I journeyed into Purgatory, my attention focused not on my surroundings but on the departed souls themselves, males and females indistinguishable one from the other, roaming in large crowds. They all looked alike because of their suffering, sorrowful countenance. When they spotted me, they rushed towards me. Like beggars do, they clung on to me; some voluntarily giving me their name. I recognized one of them, who desperately asked me for help. He had been a very distinguished and famous personality while on earth, much admired by the world. I then realized that fame, prestige, riches and glamour are only temporary things that one might enjoy for a while on earth, but they do not lead us to Paradise.

Other souls approached me who had given me many problems and sorrows while on earth. They gave me their names, asking me to forgive them and to pray for them. I would later learn how important it is not to keep a grudge against those who have died. In a mysterious way we 'hold them back' and they suffer if we do not forgive them. We keep them from the higher realms; they seem to remain chained and do not reach Heaven. We must forgive them.

As these souls surrounded me and begged for prayers, in spite of my utter helplessness, with painful effort I did as they asked. Then all of a sudden as though with one voice, the souls exhorted me to sprinkle them with holy water. Completely taken aback, I asked,

'Holy water – what for?'

'Just do it for us, please.'

I sighed, not quite understanding. Just as I was asking myself where I could find holy water, they all cried out,

'Go to the church to get some for us.'

It was as though they had read my thoughts.

I was really in no state to go to fetch holy water from the nearby church. 'Why do they want holy water?' I was perplexed. But they begged me even more, and as I realized they would not leave me alone, I dragged myself out to the road and walked to the church across from our house. There I found a priest and rushed over and asked him, 'Can I please have some holy water to take home? There are those souls, you know, *"the dead"* who want me to sprinkle some water on them.'

I waited for him to fall apart laughing at me, but at that stage of my suffering I really didn't care what he thought. I was surprised when instead he said, 'All right, I'll give you some. It is in our Catholic tradition to do so.'

He gave me a small bottle containing holy water and I walked home briskly to face the souls. Logically I could not see how to do this. Here I was, experiencing the souls of dead people, immaterial, just spirit. How was I going to sprinkle water on them, physical water that would fall to the ground? So I asked, 'How am I to sprinkle water on you since you are immaterial spirits?'

'Sprinkle the water on us with the intention that it is for us!' they answered. So I did just that.

Had they physically materialized, I would have been crushed in a stampede. Crowds came rushing towards me, wanting one simple drop of holy water to fall on them. I had plenty, so I continued sprinkling and sprinkling. For a moment it seemed as though all of Purgatory was stampeding towards me to receive just a drop of this holy water! And to my amazement, I saw many of them whooshing upwards, like shooting stars being sucked up towards heaven. They were so happy!

The funny thing was, as these souls were being relieved of their sufferings, I was still enduring the pain of feeling abandoned by God. Of course I took advantage of their presence to ask them if they had seen my Angel or the One that I had begun to love to folly, but they would give me no reply and dissipated in the fog just as they had appeared.

Perhaps God had allowed me to feel how the souls that are in Purgatory suffer from being separated from God. Whatever the reason, my spiritual drought continued. Every day that passed seemed like a year. Despite the busy world around me, I continued to feel desperately alone.

I continued to cry out, but my voice only echoed back to me.

Finally, I could bear it no longer. I wailed pathetically like a new-born baby. I raised my eyes towards Heaven and with all my might I cried out surrendering,

'Father! Where are You? Why did You leave me? Take me and do with me as You wish! Purify me, and use me, if this is Your wish!'

I finally abandoned myself *entirely* to His Will.

And then, in the blink of an eye, Heaven opened and a Voice full of emotion cried,

> *'I, God, love you! Come! Let Me rejoice always hearing these words of total surrender.'*

These words were like a balm pouring on these impressive wounds my soul had received in the desert, healing me instantly. Like a bolt of lightning shot out from Heaven, God descended with delight to reach me and raise me to His Heart, then as swift as an arrow, He cast me out once more from His embrace into the messy world we are in. At the same time, however, God compensated me by opening the Gates to Heaven, allowing me access to His inner Courts, to step in and out any time I wished.

Having surrendered thus to God, my soul, freshly filled with Heavenly dew, praised Him. I glorified Him with such words:

'Yahweh visited me! Like a gust of wind His Spirit lifted me and showed me His Countenance! He revealed to me tenderness, love, and infinite goodness. He then showered me with blessings and offered me Manna in abundance to share It with my brothers. He walked with me in the land of oblivion; from down among the dead He took me; among those who have forgotten Him He raised me, restoring the memory of my soul. O Lord, Yahweh, how grateful I am! May Your Sweetness, O Lord, be on us all. Blessed be Yahweh for ever and ever.'[2]

When I finally accepted to live God's law of love, putting God first in my life, and living a *true life in Him*, the Lord approached me and revealed to me, as well as to the whole world, the depths of His jealous Love:

> *'I love you to jealousy; I want you all Mine; I want everything you do to be for Me; I do not tolerate rivals; I want you to*

---

2 January 16, 1992

worship Me and live for Me; breathe for Me; love for Me; eat for Me; smile for Me; immolate yourself for Me; everything you will do, do it for Me; I want to consume you; I want to inflame you desiring Me only; adorn Me with your petals, My flower; crown Me with your love ... fragrance Me with your fragrance;'[3]

'allow Me to educate you and strengthen you. I want to form you into My barefoot Athlete to race with Me around the world, to go to My people and wake them up from their lethargy, pull the dead from their graves and turn them into Cathedrals.'

'Wow!' I exclaimed. This *is* serious, are we that bad? Dead? Putrefying? I mean, decomposing like rotten fruit? Is this true? Is this a warning? Is this why God speaks?

I knew that when He talked to me, He talked to each one of us. Even I, in my spiritual immaturity, knew that God would not take the trouble to come and speak to us unless things were really disastrous and the world was really in bad shape. He would not just come nonchalantly with His hands behind His back to ask us, 'Hello, creatures, how are things today? All well with you, eh? Need anything? Just give Me a call, I'm right here.'

God made me feel right in the middle of my heart that He is giving us a last chance to shape up – if we don't, He will ship us all out!

Then on December 15, 1986, as if it were nothing, God asked me,

'Daughter, do you want Wisdom?'

'Yes.'

Not realizing the value of what was being offered, I simply replied, 'Yes.' But then I came to my senses. Wisdom? Wasn't that the gift of Solomon? When God saw that I understood what He was offering, He said:

'You will have to acquire Wisdom, but I will help you.'

---

3 May 5, 1987

I saw that I would have to *earn* it. I did not know how, but God had said that He would help me. Much later I understood that Wisdom needs self-sacrifice, self-giving, immolation, accepting criticism even to be beaten black and blue without uttering a complaint, and following God's Will.

God's generosity did not stop there, for He said,

> *'I will give you the gift of discernment, the gift of fortitude and the gift of knowledge. I will give you all these gifts so long as you follow Me and do My Will.'*

The marathon with God was just starting. My Angel had said I was going to be educated by God Himself in His Celestial Courts to bear witness to an unbelieving world, a dying world. He said I would be racing like an athlete, without stopping and without resting. I knew then that I would have to rely on God's armor, for it would not be against human enemies that I would have to struggle, but against the Sovereignties and the Powers who originate the darkness in this world, the spiritual army of evil in the heavens.[4]

The race began.

---

4 Ephesians 6: 12–13

4

Angels or Demons?

I quickly saw I had an adversary who was determined to see I would never reach the finish line.

The experiences of evil in my earlier years would pale in comparison to what I was about to encounter. I was getting a crash course in the realms of the supernatural, and the dark side would now have its day.

To many people nowadays, the whole idea of the devil is a medieval construct – a horned creature with cloven hooves, depicted in cartoons or in paintings in churches or art galleries – something to laugh at, or a silly superstition. But you must understand that two invisible armies surround us. The comforting news is that the army of Good Angels is much stronger than the army of the fallen angels. Our struggle is not against flesh and blood but against Principalities and Powers. But we should never forget that God is far more powerful and stronger than Evil and He definitively conquered Satan in our world through His Son's suffering on the Cross when Jesus refused to stop loving us right into death – which is what Satan was trying to get Him to do.

And with that, God took the most tragic event in human history and turned it into the greatest triumph. He conquered all of human history from the beginning to the End of Time so that in the end it will be revealed how Satan has been the loser all the time. And the events, which we thought were so tragic, turned out to be His greatest victories.

Our Guardian Angels are like sentinels that never leave our side; wherever you go they come along, but at the same time, they never leave from the presence of God either, as they are able to bilocate or multilocate.

The devil sometimes will carry out his evil actions with subtlety so as not to be exposed. At other times he will show his hatred and jealousy quite openly and with violence, until the supernatural force subdues him. When he is defeated he usually acts imprudently: he surfaces and shows himself. It is known, however, that Satan achieves his best results when he works silently, without giving any open signals of his evil intentions or of his presence. His trickeries become more effective and have better results for him when he works under cover and avoids open confrontation. When he works without creating 'ripples on the surface of the water' that does not mean that there are no treacherous undercurrents.

So often, in our modern, digital, scientific and technical world, when we declare that the devil exists and is indeed an evil spirit, we are told that we hold old-fashioned beliefs: just theories from the Middle Ages. The devil, however, has managed to convince many learned men of his non-existence and there are some scientists who would like to prove that the devil does not exist. This alone just shows how naïve one can be. How can these good people believe that they, in a scientific manner, could examine a dark spirit who is a million times smarter than they and lives in perverted, spiritual darkness? How could they possibly prove that he does not exist? What will the devil do? He will deceive them even more by pretending he is not there! His power of dissimulation is his most effective weapon. One can learn only through personal experience and this is one more reason I am writing this book.

Each natural weakness that can lead to the regions of darkness is like a magnet that can attract demons to us. Satan is also a strategist capable of using many different methods to catch us off guard.

Very often Satan uses people for his purpose. Out of nothing at all he can produce an act of accusation to utterly ruin the one he wants to strike. But this is not all; one of his most malicious acts is to *suggest* in the 'sleeping' soul all sorts of ideas that lead the soul into a state of agitation and total unrest, wrenching all peace from within that soul. This is why we must stay alert and not allow him to find us 'sleeping'.

I'm not trying to scare you. I'm just sharing my own experiences, so you can learn, as I did, how to protect yourself from evil, relying on God's power, which is far greater than the devil's as I said before.

From my childhood, evil had been manifesting itself to me in various ways. Not only did I have the recurring visions of the hands trying to strangle me, I had also seen many times a growling black dog with red eyes, ready to pounce on me and tear me to pieces.

Somehow the devil must have known that God had a special purpose for me. But before this period in my life, I had never fully understood how powerful the devil is, and how he and his demons are constantly at work around us.

Since I had now surrendered my life to God, I had become a threat to the forces of evil, like every person who follows God. It's as if a siren goes off in Hell when a person turns to God, and that person is now on the devil's radar. Why? Because a holy person can change the world and thwart many of the devil's plans.

And so it was that shortly after my encounters with my Angel and my surrender to God, all Hell broke loose – literally.

Satan attacked me in all his fury.

As he approached me, it was the exact opposite experience of Daniel's approach. When Daniel had come to me, I felt joy and peace, when he had told me, 'God is near you and loves you.' But now as Satan approached, I immediately sensed hatred and cruelty and I heard his harsh voice yell, 'Gooooooo!'

I guessed that meant 'Go', and that he was saying I should stop speaking with my Angel and God. I didn't know much about the devil, but there was no mistaking the malevolence in his harsh voice. It was terrifying. His presence startled me. I experienced the most awful feelings of dread, making me freeze with fear and the heavy weight of evil all around me accompanied by an awful stench of sulfur filling the air.

The devil's growl sounded more like a wild animal than a person. It reverberated and for the first time in my life, I felt a chill shoot up from my lower back all the way to my head. I searched within myself to find Daniel and God once more, but they seemed to have withdrawn.

Then the voice thundered again, 'Gooooo! Withdraw from here you bitch! Withdraw, or else fire in Hell does the rest!'

Summoning all my strength, and calling to God in my soul, I answered with the single word, 'No!' implying that I would not withdraw from either Daniel or God. The devil cried out that I was cursed and that my soul was damned, and he continued shouting obscenities as he took the shape of a madman, continuously berating and tormenting me.

He accused me of every sort of evil. (I learned later that the devil bears another name, the 'accuser', because on Judgment Day, he will accuse us of every sin we have committed while Jesus will be justifying us.) Just as God is all love, all compassion and all understanding, the devil is exactly the opposite. As he attacked me, his insults were so powerful I thought I would lose my mind.

Such attacks happened during the day and also even more fearfully at night. It was almost impossible for me to sleep. It also felt as if the devil was trying to squeeze all the breath out of my body; as though an eagle had put its claws on my stomach, gripped it, and tried to choke me. It was a very real, physical sensation.

As this torment continued, I began to cry, and the devil scornfully mocked me saying, 'Stop watering your wounds!'

Underneath my own absolute horror I sensed that behind my struggle there was another great battle going on between the devil and my Angel Daniel, who was fighting hard on my behalf. I knew that without supernatural help, I would not survive. I began to call on my Angel, and he uttered just one word in reply: 'Pray.' So I prayed with my whole being, begging God for help.

Finally, after some time, the battle ended. The devil ceased his attack and I was able to get a few days' peace. In those still and peaceful moments, I began to think about how important my Guardian Angel was. I knew he was fighting for me, keeping him away, as a good friend, caring for me, and protecting me. And I needed his protection because the devil doesn't give up easily, and he was preparing new and different attacks.

First, the devil turned his attention to my family. My niece, who is my goddaughter, waited fifteen years before sharing her nightmare with me. She saw herself sitting at the head of a long dining table and around her neck hung several rosaries. There were others at the table and I too was sitting at the far end. Suddenly the door opened, Satan stepped in and went over to her. She described him as half goat, from the waist down, and half human, with an ugly face and huge curved horns on his head. While describing her nightmare, she burst into tears, sobbing very hard as she recalled the horror of that sight and his threatening words,

'I hate your aunt and I hate you, as well!'

Something similar happened to my son in his sleep when the devil appeared to him as a very old man with a long beard. In that dream, the devil said to him,

'You, tell your mom to stop writing; otherwise I'll do the same to you as I did to her when she was very young. I'll put my hands around your neck and strangle you!'

I had never told my son about those nightmares of mine, so it was clear that it was the devil.

These attacks really worried me. To make sure the devil would not be allowed to attack my family, I asked the Lord to intervene. So He promised me He would appoint St Michael the Archangel as our Guardian; with that guarantee I felt better.

Next, the devil tried a different way to influence me. Cunning as he is, and knowing I was still very uneducated about the spirit world, the devil assumed the likeness of my own Angel Daniel.

This false angel tried to fool me by presenting to me a different image of the loving God and caring Father I knew on the day I had said the Lord's Prayer to Him.

This false angel started telling me that God was a fearful presence and that I should be afraid of Him. Satan's aim was to draw me away from God and His plans for me. He made God sound very frightening, trying to put me in such fear of God, so that when He did come and speak to me I would be fearful of His call. At times there were moments when I found it almost impossible to distinguish between the voice of Daniel and that of the devil. This false angel led me to believe that God was short-tempered, quick to anger and a terrible judge who would punish His people for the slightest fault. For a while I began to believe him.

A little later, the devil took on the likeness of my deceased father, and his voice sounded exactly like him. This 'impression' of my father spoke to me in French, as my father often did. He told me that God had sent him to tell me that my communications with God were all an illusion. He said, 'God, speaking to you! Where did you ever hear of such a thing before?' He said this could only mean I was crazy.

I suspected something was strange about this vision, so I said, 'Well what about Daniel? Is it possible that Angels can appear to us?'

'Oh that one,' he replied, and his voice then filled with such hatred that I immediately recognized it was the devil trying to trick me. My father would never have spoken to me in such a way.

During this interlude I started to feel very much alone. There in Bangladesh at that time I had nobody to turn to for advice or spiritual help. I didn't want to worry my husband by explaining what was taking place. I kept everything to myself. The devil knew all this, so he increased his attacks. Each day he brought more and more demons with him. Day and night I could both feel and hear them around me. These fallen angels attacked me, mocked me and called me all sorts of obscene names. I wondered why God was allowing me to go through all of this.

But eventually, the mental torment I was going through no longer had the same effect on me. I knew that God was stronger than the devil. And the closer I came to God, the less I feared Satan, and he trembled all the more, wanting my death. His rage increased, and accordingly he changed his strategy once again.

The devil now began to *physically* attack me. I can't fully explain how this happened, as it was part physical and part spiritual.

First, the devil splashed boiling oil on my hand. I had been writing down all the messages from God and my Angel, and this oil burned the middle finger of my right hand, creating a terrible blister exactly where I held my pencil. I had to apply a protective dressing each day just to hold the pencil and continue my communications with Daniel and God.

On another occasion, during a family holiday in Thailand, we decided to take a trip over to one of the islands, but on the way back the boat juddered as we approached the shore. I lost my balance and to steady myself I grabbed at whatever was closest to me. It turned out to be the red-hot exhaust pipe of the boat's engine. The whole palm of my right hand was badly burned and came on top of the oil burn I had received earlier. My hand was unbearably painful and all the way back to the hotel I worried that it might require hospital treatment. It seemed certain that it would be many days – even weeks – before I could hold a pencil again.

Despite what appeared to be an awful burn, by the time we entered our hotel again I had absolutely no pain in my hand. What's more, the redness and in fact any sign of the burn had disappeared.

God would only allow the devil to go so far and in His mercy, He had healed my hand!

Sometimes the devil will use those very things we most hate. One of my greatest horrors is of cockroaches. Even telling this story is horrible for me, but it shows just how evil and hateful the devil can be. At home one day, as I left a room I pulled the door shut behind me. Almost immediately I felt wetness on my face where some sort of liquid had sprayed me. Instantly, I heard the voice of the devil laughing as he said,

'This is the way I baptize.'

It was then that I realized I had squashed flat a really big cockroach between the door and the frame. The liquid that sprayed me was its substance. I can't tell you how much this incident disgusted me, but it shows how the devil will go to any lengths to take his revenge and scare us into turning away from our rightful path and from God.

The picture started to become clearer to me: Satan wanted to absolutely discourage me from conversing with God. This was a major spiritual battle.

God also showed me that it was specifically because I had returned to Him that the devil was now attacking me. So long as I was not fully with God, the devil was not disturbed. But the devil had become enraged when he saw that God was training and forming me to fight against evil.

One night I saw a vision. I was standing in a room and I saw a snake slithering by. This snake represented the devil. I knew this snake was my pet, and that I was neglecting it and no longer feeding it. Hungry, and astonished, it crept out of its hole in search of food. I watched it slithering towards its dish where it found a couple of grapes. The snake swallowed them but did not seem satisfied, so it crawled towards the kitchen in search of food. In the meantime it sensed that I had changed my feeling towards it and now I had become its enemy instead of its friend. I recognized this instinctively and knew that it would soon turn on me and try to kill me. I was frightened.

Just then my Guardian Angel appeared and asked what was troubling me. I told him about the snake, and how worried I felt now that I had become its enemy. My Angel said he would help me get rid of it. I hesitated, though, wondering whether I should join him in the battle or not but I decided that I should join my Angel and do the work together.

Daniel took a broom and opened a door that led outside. Then he went to the snake and with the broom frightened it toward the open door. The snake slithered all around to avoid the broom, trying to climb up on cupboards, and on shelves. In the end, due to my Angel's powerful presence, it slithered out of the door and my Angel slammed the door behind it. Together we watched from the window how the snake reacted. It panicked. We saw it heading back again towards the door, but the door was safely shut. Not knowing where to go, we saw it speeding down the staircase and out into the street. The minute it had slithered across the threshold of the main entrance into the cold it transformed itself into a gigantic toad (a size bigger than a human being) and again it took the shape of an evil spirit. The alarm was given and the people, who were just out there, caught the evil spirit and tied it up.

This vision was given to me after I had accepted God and had surrendered entirely to Him.

A few days later as I was going down the staircase at home leading to the kitchen, at the landing of the staircase, I suddenly saw Jesus. He was smiling at me and I noticed that He had dimples on His cheeks; He appeared to be quite content, happy and by the look in His eyes

He was manifesting His love to me. I stood there staring, then He disappeared. Up until that point, my Angel and God the Father had approached me, but now I had seen Jesus Christ Himself!

I suddenly remembered the dreams I had as a child with Jesus, but now here was He, smiling again at me. Later that afternoon He appeared and introduced Himself.

> *'I am the Sacred Heart. In the middle of My Heart, have a place, My beloved, there you will live.'*

And then He vanished, but not for long. Later He came back again and said:

> *'Peace be with you. I want you to write all of this down ... I want My children to understand that their souls live and that evil exists; all that is written in My Blessed Word is not a myth; Satan exists and seeks to ruin your souls ...'*[1]

No sooner were these words pronounced than I found myself underground. I did not fall into a trance, as this vision was given to me in my intellect.

The area I found myself in was similar to an underground cave, with a low 'ceiling', dark, with only the light shed by the fire. It felt damp and the ground was dark gray and sticky as though wet, but the texture of the 'soil' was extremely fine, like flour.

In front of me I saw several souls, tied up in a row. I saw only their heads. The rest of their body was behind a 'wall'. Their faces looked like masks of agony. I then realized there was noise around me. It sounded like the noise of heavy iron machines at work, clamor and hammering, and all around me the the damned could be heard moaning and shrieking. I had the impression that it was a very busy place.

I saw that Satan was standing about five meters in front of me with his back to me, while facing the damned. His outstretched hand was full of burning hot lava, and he waved his arm from right to left, splashing the lava across the faces of the damned, scorching them and causing their faces to swell. He sensed there was someone behind

---

1 March 7, 1987

him, and turned around to look at me. His face resembled a human face, but it showed absolute anger and hatred especially in his eyes. He looked like a madman.

As soon as he saw me he spat on the ground with disgust. With a harsh coarse voice that sounded more like a growl than a voice he said:

'Look at her! Miserable worm, look at her! We even have worms nowadays coming to suck out our blood. Go and f … off!'

Then, with evil joy, he said to me,

'Look!'

Again he threw lava across those faces while they moaned and shrieked with agony. I heard them cry out:

'Oh let us die …'

Then, Satan fuming with rage called out:

'Creatures of the earth, hear me. To me you will come!'

Although he was shrieking out his threats, I thought, 'What a fool he is to believe that he will win in the end …' He must have guessed what I was thinking, because he said in a menacing tone,

'I am not a fool!'

Then with a malicious laugh and with irony he shouted at those poor souls,

'Have you heard? She called me a fool. Dearly beloved souls, I will make you pay for her sayings.'

As he was about to take new lava to throw, I turned to Jesus in despair and asked Him to do something to stop him. Jesus said,

'I will stop him.'

The moment Satan lifted his arm to throw the lava it gave him so much pain that he screeched, cursing Jesus and then he shouted at me,

'Witch! Go! Yes go! Leave us!'

Suddenly there was the sound of voices coming from souls standing just outside the gates of Hell – the lowest Purgatory, but not in Hell. Aware of our presence they cried desperately to us,

'Save us, save us!'

Then out of nowhere, someone came forward to Satan; I understood it was one of his demons. I believe Satan could no longer see us, as he carried on as though we weren't there. He said to the demon,

'Are you about your duty? Are you doing what I have asked you to do? Hurt her; destroy her, discourage her.'

Satan's orders to that demon were intended for me. He wanted that demon to be at my heels to discourage me and destroy my mission.

Satan began to call out the names of other demons, and I heard human names as well. I then realized that damned souls in Hell could also possess people and create demonic trouble for us since they are under the dominion of Lucifer, and anyone under him lives in hate. They don't, however, have the immense power of the fallen angels. I asked Jesus if we could leave this place and He said,

> *'Come let us leave. I want you to write all of this down.'*

I realized, after this vision, how Jesus is completely dominant over Satan. Jesus instructed me that I should use His Name to cast demons away. This gave me peace and confidence.

Soon after this vision of Hell, Satan sent a whole group of demons to attack me. With my new confidence, I sarcastically said, 'Oh, no, not again,' knowing that I would be able to handle them this time.

These demons were small in shape and resembled chimpanzees. They pounced on my back like furious cats. But I felt secure, stronger than they were, and no longer afraid of them, just tired of them. I felt deep in my soul that I could just wipe them out by using the Name of Jesus. They were more of a nuisance than a danger, like flies buzzing around food. Fed up with them, I ordered them to return to Hell, using the Name of Jesus. Whimpering, the demons left immediately!

5

The Spirit World

At this point, I started to share more and more of my experiences with a small circle of friends. I was relieved that they actually believed what I was telling them. I told them of my Angel and the approach of God, and most of them thought the whole thing was amazing. So I started explaining to them everything I had learned so far. And since the attacks of Satan were so fresh on my mind, I talked about him.

'We barely notice the devil around us,' I explained. 'We might think of him when we read about some horrendous crime, but for most of us, the devil appears to leave us alone. We go our own way and live the lives we wish, oblivious to the fact that just as there is a power for good in creation, there is also a power for evil.'

One of my friends said that he thought evil was just the result of people doing evil things and creating 'hell' around us.

I replied that the devil's latest trick in our times is to pretend he – and Hell – do not exist. For that very reason, our Lord had shown me the vision of Hell, so that I would be able to testify to its existence. When a man once told St Padre Pio that he did not believe in Hell, the saint replied dryly, 'You will believe it when you are there!'

One of my friends asked, 'What about the fallen angels, are they the same as the demons?'

'Yes they are, and they too will be judged severely in that Day of Judgment. God gave me a vision to see them while they were proceeding forward towards His Throne to receive their judgment. I remember in that terrible Day that there was an eerie silence hanging in the air and everything was still. All the souls that were saved and deserved Heaven were standing all around the area leaving a wide-open space in the center. Then from the other end of that wide area I saw a great multitude of these fallen angels moving slowly forward, while dragging their feet with their heads bent down. This sight was both awesome and sad. They looked like soldiers who had lost a war and had been taken prisoners to be judged, without any power left in them.'

Here is the Message God gave revealing this vision:

> *'My angels who had been given supreme authority rebelled against Me and destruction took the best out of them. My Justice did not spare them; they were thrown down to the underworld to wait for the Day of Judgment; they too will be judged before the very eyes of everyone; and ah! ... What a terrible sight that will be! I will judge everyone according to what he has done and not done; in front of My Throne everyone will stand in silence and in awe for the Day of this final Judgment will be so dreadful that it will make everyone tremble with fright in front of the Supreme Judge that I Am.*
>
> *'You will all see a huge number of fallen angels who were driven out of Heaven and fought in bitterness and spite against Michael the Archangel and his Angels. Yes. Yes, your eyes will see My Rivals, the Rivals of the Holy One, of the Anointed One; you will all see those fallen angels, adepts of Lucifer, the primeval serpent who tried to lead My sons and My daughters all astray; you will see multitudes of those who defiled My Name and transgressed My Law; those who refused to be reared and fostered by My Holiness and preferred to be labeled on their forehead by the Deceiver; Vassula, a harsh vision has been shown you.'*[1]

Satan, whose name was Lucifer when he was still an Angel, rebelled against God; his rebellion affected a third of the Angels in Heaven, and when they fell, Hell was created as their abode. Hell is their domain, and it is real.

---

1 July 20, 1992

People these days often ignore the existence of God, but they also fail to realize the very real power of the devil and his demons. This power of evil hates us to be in direct communion with God, and he will do anything to prevent God's Will from being done on earth.

One of my friends interrupted and said, 'But how can we sense that he is there, present in a situation?'

'You have to be on your guard,' I answered. 'He can take anything, even small things, and work through them. He is a great strategist and a legalist. If he finds an opening in us, either from our sinfulness or our weaknesses, as a legalist he will claim that he has every right to do his dirty business in us and through us, because sin is his domain. Sin gives a foothold to Satan. Corrupting our body and giving way to insidious acts of rebellion are openings for an evil encounter.'

Another friend asked, obviously not understanding, 'What foothold?'

I repeated,

'Sins; everyday sins, lack of charity, hardness of heart, lack of forgiving, pride, hostility, slander, prejudice, arrogance and so on, not to mention sins like stealing, lying, cheating, adultery, killing, etc. In his cunning Satan is, as I have said, a legalist and where he finds a foothold he will say, "Aha, these are my favorite sins and now I have the legal right to abide in these regions for they are mine!"

'For example, if within a family there is a lack of forgiveness, a lack of love and prayer, these can be openings for evil spirits to create disruption and cause division in relationships. Much of the strife in families is caused because we've given the devil a foothold in our homes. Without prayer, our homes and our families can be easily invaded, but so can our bodies. I've heard so many people brag that their body is their own, and they can do whatever they wish with it. But we forget that we are not just body, but soul and spirit as well. Our body is actually the *sanctuary* of the Holy Spirit and His abode.'

With these words, one of my friends turned away and I could see she started to weep. I asked her what was wrong, and she explained that some time ago she had had an abortion. I'm sure she was not the only one in the room who had been affected by this sin, as it is so prevalent today. I said to her, and to everyone else, 'Listen, your sins can be forgiven if you truly repent of them.' They nodded in understanding.

At this point I opened the book containing the Messages and read out to them the following passage:

'I asked Jesus, "Will you forgive me?" Jesus replied, *"O Vassula, I forgive you, write what you saw."* I wrote: His divine Face lit with a bright smile showing me His dimples and opening His arms wide open so that I fall in them.

> *"Forgiveness will always be given without the slightest hesitation, and I made you discern Me fully so that you are able to tell My children the way I forgive."*[2]

'Satan wants to accuse you of your sins, and lead you to despair. He will even use other people to condemn you. He'll create accusations against you that are not even true. All of this is to lead you to despair, agitation and unrest – to make you think, "Well, I'm bad, I'm a sinner, so who cares?"

'But God wants to offer you His forgiveness. God is doing everything possible to offer you His love, and His redemption. The Heart of Jesus trembles with love. It is sad to see how many people do not understand that the Kingdom of God is among us; not just in an apparition of Jesus or of the Virgin Mary.

'We all long for Heaven and should work with a spirit of detachment to earthly activities but the fact is that God has us here on earth for a reason so that our souls might be formed in Him in faith to the point where the emptiness of the tomb that we feel on this earth only helps us believe more fully that He is truly risen.

'We have been given too many signs of the supernatural to ignore them and turn away from them – signs given to "normal" people, not to lunatics. Now is the time to recognize these signs, and give our lives to God.'

At that point, the room was quiet as we all thought about what this meant. I could tell the words were getting through.

Sometime later I had another experience with a friend who finally came face to face with the reality of sin in her life – in a most bizarre and disturbing way.

2 December 6, 1987

I invited her over to give her some advice, as I knew she had started to take a dangerous path in her life. I told her, 'You have to decide whether you want to carry on your way or change. You must keep away from those friends who are influencing you to do bad things. They are dragging you away from the right path. Can't you see?'

At first she resisted. I knew this would not be easy for her. I went over to the fridge to get a bottle of soda to drink, and filled both our glasses. She was still not going to talk about her sins, and was ready to start denying them and lie to me. But at that very moment, God revealed to me all the wrong she was doing, so that I could correct her and advise her. As I was revealing her sins, she was in shock, and tears started to stream down her cheeks.

After a while, we had emptied our glasses. As I was refilling them, we suddenly both saw maggots in her glass! They just suddenly appeared – hundreds of them, crawling in the soda. We saw them distinctly since the soda was a dark color and contrasted sharply with the white maggots. It was disgusting.

But I knew exactly what had happened. It was a sign. I said to her, 'Do you know what this is? This is one of Satan's signatures. When you expose him he gives you his signature, his seal, and maggots are one of his seals. I uncovered your sins but in truth it was the devil that was being revealed. He has been laying traps for you and now in his anger and vindictiveness he shows it in this way.' I knew this woman would never forget this day!

Later I had another experience that helped me understand how the devil operates in our lives and how God rescues us from evil. A good friend of mine had been having trouble with her parents for a long time. They were constantly rejecting her and for years she had felt their hostility. This hatred and bitterness between them had allowed the devil to enter into their home. My friend ended up jobless and homeless, so I invited her to stay with us until she could stand on her own feet.

One day I invited her to join me on a trip that was going near her mother's house. I suggested she could bring her mother some presents. As soon as we arrived in her mother's town, she called her, but received a cold and uncharitable response. My friend had to plead with her mother to be allowed to go to her house and give her the presents. At first her mother had flatly refused, but she finally accepted on the condition that the gifts were to be left on the doorstep, insisting she would not invite her daughter into the house.

So we drove to her mother's house, parked on the opposite side of the road and saw her waiting for us outside. I dared not approach since I knew she liked neither me nor her daughter. When she spotted us, however, she made signs for us to go over and come inside. I went in while my friend went back and forth fetching her gifts.

The lady poured out her problems to me while preparing coffee, telling me how her son had distanced himself from her and her husband. I listened patiently to her family problems.

Finally, the three of us sat down at a small table and drank our coffee together. The table was below a window facing the courtyard, and while she was talking I clearly saw several demons jumping out of that window, fleeing the house. They all had the appearance of ugly chimpanzees, and they knew it was time to leave.

After that meeting, peace came into that house and the parents not only became reconciled with their daughter, loving her once more, but also were appreciative of my act of charity towards their daughter, calling me 'a second mother'. The hatred that had given the devil a foothold was now replaced with love, which is the sign of the Holy Spirit's workings.

Another time, I saw five evil spirits on a man who was an alcoholic. I saw the demon who had helped turn this man into an alcoholic, and I saw that the other four were the spirits of anger, grudge, stubbornness, and pride. They were all tormenting him and would not leave him. I saw them climbing all over him like chimpanzees, and though he was frantically trying to push them away, there were too many for him to deal with alone. Here I must point out that this vision was given to me in spite of this person being in another country.

I knew this person was in danger and wanted to warn him, so I phoned his office. But his secretary said he was not in and suggested I call again later. I then called every day, but I was never able to reach him. After a few days I learned that he had fallen gravely ill, mainly from alcohol related problems. Tragically, he soon died.

The devil hates prayer and feels uncomfortable while prayer is going on. This is another story of exorcism.

Once, in Brazil, where a crowd of 26,000 people had gathered in a stadium hall to hear my witnessing and pray together with them, a possessed man was present. The Bishop in attendance has never forgotten the following incident that took place. As soon as I began to share my experiences with God and read out to them the Messages, the possessed man, who was perched quite high up in the stand, started to shout out like a hundred loudspeakers:

'I don't want to hear God's words anymore! I know you come from God and I suffer when I hear them!'

He was about to throw himself down from that considerable height. Suddenly, the entire crowd, being charismatic Christians, and as though they were all programmed, turned spontaneously with their hands raised towards him, and prayed for his deliverance. The man dropped to the ground with a sudden thud on the hard floor and lay inert for some time. After a while as we were still praying over him, he got up, a bit shaken, and looked around him bewildered, as if coming out from sleep, and again after a few minutes, he lifted his arms up high and started to praise God for His Mercy and for having delivered him from the demon. Prayers and worship keep the demons away. The Lord permitted this incident to remind us that the devils exist and that there is always a way to be delivered from them through prayer.

One day, after a successful retreat in Colombia, just before leaving for the airport, I went to say goodbye to a small group of people seated at a table having just finished their lunch. As I approached, a young lady in the group abruptly stood up and backed away, covering her face with her hands. Shaking like a leaf she ran away to the corner of the hall, her face still hidden. I went over to the corner, approaching her slowly, at first not understanding the young lady's strange reaction and gently touched her on the shoulder. She whimpered as though burned by the touch and trembling with fear she crouched down as low as possible, wanting to disappear. Then I understood: the demon inside her was afraid of me. I deeply regretted that because of my plane departure time I could not stay to pray over her and cast out the demon. I therefore turned to a charismatic friend who had seen everything, and knowing that he had dealt with demons before I asked him:

'You know what you are supposed to do, don't you?'

'Yes, I'll deal with it.'

Feeling reassured I left for the airport. On the way there, however, a thought came to me: I knew that Satan is a liar and a comedian too. I knew too of my weaknesses and that I was far from being holy, so how could it be that he feared me as much as he showed? Could it be that he was putting on this act for me so that I would start thinking that I am somebody important and so holy that it doesn't need more than my mere presence to drive the demons berserk? Did he want to make me fall into temptation and pride? So I settled with this theory: he pretended to be scared of me …

God gave me this Message:

> *'Today more than ever, the evil one and the demons are roaming in every corner of this earth, seeking to deceive you all, setting traps for you to fall into; this is the reason why I am asking you to pray without ceasing; do not let My adversary find you asleep; be on your guard these days; do not let him find an empty corner in you either, fill yourselves with My Word, with My Love, with My Peace, with My Virtues; come often and receive Me*[3] *in purity so that you do not yield into temptation; pray without ceasing; I know your needs even more than you do and even before you ask Me, I know your heart; in every possible occasion face Me and pray …'*[4]

God has given us a powerful weapon to protect us against the devil, and that weapon is prayer.

These experiences were a great awakening for me as I began to grasp the meaning of the angelic powers of good and evil, and the spirit world.

As the sacred communications progressed there were perceptible changes in me in the growth of knowledge and love for God.

---

3 The Eucharist

4 April 5, 1989

6

Confrontation

As a result of all that was happening to me I started to go to a church nearby. It was Roman Catholic, and though I was Greek Orthodox, the Catholic church was the closest to my home – only a few blocks away. After a few days my Angel asked me to go to the seminary on the church premises to look for an American priest who lived there. I was to tell him about my supernatural experiences and show the Messages I had carefully written in notebooks.

It was dusk as I walked through the garden at the seminary. I saw a man carrying a plastic bucket of washed, dry clothes. He seemed surprised to see me at such an hour and asked if I was looking for somebody. 'An American priest,' I said. He replied that he would be back shortly, and asked me if I wished to wait in his cell.

He introduced himself as Fr. Karl, and as we walked into his cell I began to tell him of my experiences and confidently I showed him the Messages. Being naïve in these matters, I expected him to rejoice with me. Instead, he tilted his head and lowered it, and his words to me indicated he thought I was going through a psychological crisis, or suffering from schizophrenia. He asked me where my husband was and I told him he was away in Europe for a while. He must have deduced I was so miserable and unhappy being alone in Asia, that I had lost my mind. He asked if he could see the palms of my hands, and as he studied them I knew he was trying to find traces of a mental disorder, as shows up in certain mental cases. He pitied me and invited me to come at any time to see him.

After that first encounter, I went over to see him every few days, determined to prove to him that I was normal. One day he asked, 'I wonder if you would allow me to see this phenomenon while you are communicating with Heaven?' I prayed silently and immediately I felt God approaching in His special way. Then God spoke to me and I positioned my hand to write what He said, but at that very moment the priest grabbed my wrist to see whether he could stop my hand from writing. At once he felt a sort of tingling current penetrating his arm and he withdrew his hand very quickly, with a look of shock on his face. He did not say anything and just watched in silence while I received the words of God.

Later on, I found out that he went over to tell Fr. Jim, the American priest, all about it, especially about the tingling, electrical feeling that stayed with him throughout the afternoon. Fr. Jim had often seen me on the premises, and when he heard of this latest experience he felt sure that it must be diabolical. He said to Fr. Karl, 'Look, do you see any trace of holiness in her? Certainly not! So her experience can't be from God. Why don't you ask her to come over to me and I will test her.'

Fr. Karl told me that Fr. Jim wanted to see me. Since the latter was convinced he was dealing with a demon, in preparation for my visit he sprinkled his room with holy water, and also sprinkled the chair I was to sit on, the desk, and the paper and pencil prepared for my use.

I went over feeling confident, but when I arrived I saw that Fr. Jim was agitated and nervous. He wanted his test to be quickly over and done, so without wasting time he asked me to call 'whatever' I was communicating with and ask 'it' to write, 'Glory be to the Father, to the Son and to the Holy Spirit.'

I prayed calmly and asked God to use my hand and write this in the special writing that He used for the Messages. And He did, but with such power that the pencil snapped in half and I had to complete it with a pen. As soon as the pencil snapped the priest jumped up, went out through the open door into the corridor and ran away. He came back rather shaken and upset and started to tell me all about the cult of Satan, evil and dumb spirits, magic, divinations, and spells. He insisted that I was communicating with a dumb spirit, certainly not one of divine origin.

He blamed Fr. Karl for believing me, saying how gullible he was. I saw that he was afraid, but even so he managed to confuse me and fill me with doubts. When I got up to leave, his manner was very aggressive and he ordered me not to come to the Catholic church premises again or attend Mass unless I stopped writing altogether. He added that I was to leave Fr. Karl alone. Shocked, I managed to tell him that Christ would never turn away anyone who loved Him, or shut the door on someone who wanted to be with Him.

Shattered by that encounter where I sensed cruelty and hardness of heart, but fear as well, I ran to see Fr. Karl on my way out, believing him to be at least gentler. I told him what had happened, saying that his friend had forbidden me to visit him and had asked me to refrain from coming to the church altogether unless I stopped writing. He bowed his head and remained silent. It was clear that Fr. Karl wasn't going to stick up for me. Perhaps he felt relieved that he'd no longer have to deal with me, and the complexity of my situation. I could see that for them I had become a nuisance, a major problem that disturbed their regular and peaceful life. I understood that I was *persona non grata.*

Before I left I told Fr. Karl, 'Yes, even I know that the devil can play tricks and we need to be careful because he is so treacherous, but the devil would never work to bring me to God and to repentance and back to the Sacraments of the Church. So how *could* it be the devil?'

What a danger for souls, I thought, to be so misguided by ignorance and such fear of the devil, thus giving him honor rather than honoring God! For several years this priest was to become such a thorn to me, followed later by others, so much so that without the consolations of God I would not have been able to continue.

I asked myself, 'How is it that they cannot see and give glory to God for the merciful graces He is giving His people? It's as if Christ has remained in the sepulchre and has never resurrected! Why do they want Him dead? Why is this mistake repeated over and over again? How is it that they can be deceived so much that they attribute works of God to Satan?'

'Great ones of the world, will your hearts always be hardened, will you never cease setting your heart on shadows, following a lie?'[1]

I became upset and found myself snapping at Fr. Karl, 'I will go! And never again will you see me here on your premises – ever!' And so I left, thinking I was leaving the Catholic church for good. I returned home and went upstairs into the bathroom. I sat facing the wall in the shower corner and cried my eyes out. My Angel came to console me, wiping away my tears and the sweat from my brow. I lamented to God just like a child that has been beaten up by a bully and runs to his father to cry its pain, so too I ran to God our Father and lamented:

'I am confused and my soul is grieving beyond anyone's imagination ... I don't know anymore ... You say it is You and You are confusing me. I believed You, because You said so with divine tenderness. I sense Your Presence around me and no one can tell me it is the devil's presence. You are perfuming all around me Your Presence, so how could it be Satan? I did not look for You, but You who found me and called me. No one, not even the whole world, had they tried to bring me to You, would have succeeded, that was how far my heart was from You. But now You, You came filling my soul with joy. My heart could not be deceived, since I felt Your sweetness on me. You poured all over me Your Name like oil to anoint me. *You have anointed me.* You lifted me restoring the memory of my soul. But look, Your very own now denies Your grace and only sees the devil. If it is truly You, my Lord, then one day I want this priest to admit it and see that my communications are of divine origin, and then I will believe fully and be in peace!'

There was just a moment's silence and God simply said with a very grave tone in His voice,

'I will bend him.'

Fr. Jim had given me three prayers to say each day. These were St Michael's Prayer, the Memorare of St Bernard and a Novena to the Sacred Heart of Jesus. Because of what had happened, I was

1 Psalms 4: 3

confused and started doubting, but something inside me told me to pray those three prayers. I repeated them every day, and did exactly what the priest had asked of me: to stop accepting the Messages from God and to stop writing them down. I felt that I had been put in prison and that someone had bound my hands and feet.

It was not long, however, before one day, as I was writing notes, I suddenly felt the power and the glory of God invading me and my hand was suddenly seized. God approached me again when I least expected it. The Message I heard filled me with the most incredible feelings of love and peace. I wrote it down:

> *'I, God, love you, daughter, always remember this. Yahweh is My Name.'*

I hadn't been looking for a Message – it simply happened when I had a pencil and paper in front of me. I was so touched, instantly bursting into tears. Then almost immediately another Message came from God:

> *'I love you Vassula, remember always this. I, it is, who am guiding you. Yahweh is My Name.'*

Amidst all the criticism and the censure, God had come to visit me in my 'prison'. It was as if the door to my prison was suddenly thrust open and a beam of celestial light filled my cell, enveloping me and filling my heart with hope. He had taken the time and the trouble – the One who holds the whole universe in the palm of His hand – to show His love and affection to me.

Even at a distance Fr. Jim could not tolerate the supernatural happenings that had surrounded me. He wrote me letters telling me that everything that had happened to me was just so much rubbish. He said I should look at myself and realize that such a grace would never be given to a person like me, because such graces were reserved for 'worthy' and deserving people, such as Mother Teresa. In some ways he seemed to be talking about himself. After so much study and so many years as a priest dedicated to Christ why shouldn't he experience such a grace? Why would God offer such a blessing to a worldly and previously unreligious person such as me? He insisted that what was happening to me was diabolical. 'It is certainly supernatural, but it is brought about by the devil, and definitely not by God.'

For a time there must have been part of me that believed Fr. Jim because after my confrontation with him every time God approached me I literally chased Him away. If in my soul I heard God say the words, '*I, Yahweh, love you,*' I would pretend not to hear Him and I wouldn't write anything down. If Jesus approached me and said, '*Peace, My child,*' I would ignore Him and try to put His words to the back of my mind, fearing that it was the devil speaking to me. I even became quite aggressive. Over and over again I refused to communicate with either God or Jesus and this might have continued even longer had it not been for my Angel Daniel.

'How could I have possibly believed that God, the Almighty, would speak and communicate with me in such a simple and direct way?' I asked myself. In my whole life I had never heard of such a thing. Of course in the Bible, people such as Moses, Abraham and the Prophets had talked to God, but what was I compared to them? How could I ever have believed it was God? It had to be an illusion. So over and over again, I refused to communicate with either God the Father or Jesus.

But in spite of these doubts and what I was being told by Fr. Jim, something inside me still trusted my Angel Daniel. He came to me one day and told me that he had a Message for me, from Jesus. He offered to be the go-between, and shared the words. Gradually my doubts abated and my wounds began to heal, and the sense of peace returned to me. As my Angel continued to visit me, he would sometimes draw for me, using my hand, pictures of himself and me, sometimes of Cathedrals, and other drawings. Then on June 20, 1986, my Angel told me he had another Message for me from Jesus. I wrote down the words without thinking and then, about to erase them because the words of the priest were still in my mind, my Angel asked me not to rub out the words but to read them. This was my first communication with Jesus since my crisis had begun. They simply read: '*I, Jesus, love you.*'

Slowly my Angel Daniel convinced me to receive more Messages. On July 9, 1986, I received a Message from God, which said,

> *'I have fed you [spiritually]. I came to give the food to you. Please help the others by giving them this food too ... Help them and lead them to Me. I have given you Love, so follow Me. I have favored you by giving you this food. Give it to the others too, to delight in it.'*

Despite my initial disappointment with the priests at the seminary, I had not lost contact with them altogether. I had stopped talking about the Messages to Fr. Jim, the one who had condemned me so brutally. However, I did tell him eventually that the Messages were still coming to me. By this time I had stopped writing down the communications on bits of paper and had started to write them in notebooks, so that they would appear in order and would not be lost. I decided to invite Fr. Jim to my house in order to tell him that I was still communicating with God. He didn't like what I had to tell him, but I gave him the notebooks to take back to the seminary to study them. The next day he sent me a very stern letter, telling me to burn the notebooks immediately and to tell those of my friends who had read some of the Messages to forget everything they had read. I was still rather inexperienced in religious matters, but had learned enough to discern the evil one.

When I told my friends his frame of mind, telling them what he said, they were both shocked and indignant. He expected me to visit him at the seminary the following day, to report back to him concerning my friends' reaction. He was rather displeased when he heard what I had to say on their behalf. I asked him to give me back my notebooks. He told me that God was probably very angry with me because I had allowed myself to be deceived in this way. He was certain that God would now abandon me to my terrible fate. He added that God had been patient with me, not once, but twice, but that now, as I would not listen, our Heavenly Father would abandon me to the devil.

I thanked God for giving me the gift of discerning spirits – a gift very useful to me at that particular moment. I had been deceived by the devil on many occasions, but it wasn't going to happen this time. I replied to Fr. Jim's harsh letter, telling him that clearly his God was not my God. The God that Fr. Jim presented to me was a cruel God, quick to anger, impatient, intolerant, lacking mercy, and lacking love. His God forgave once or twice but then turned His back on needy souls and threw them into Hell if they did not listen; whereas the God I knew, the One who spoke to me daily, was all love, infinitely patient, tolerant and tender. I told him that my God was slow to anger, all merciful, and enveloped my soul with love. My God who visits me every day in my room – the One whom he treated as if He were the devil or a dumb spirit – surrounds my soul with peace, consolation, and hope. My God, I continued, nourishes me spiritually, building my faith in Him and it is still the same today. My God teaches me spiritual things and reveals to me the riches of His Heart. He is all forgiving. He forgives every crime if we repent; this is what He says:

> *'I will not blame you for your sins. I forgive you now. I will not shut the door in your face. I tell you truly that I can forgive a million times and with My Arms open I stand before you, asking you to come to Me and feel this love I have to give you ... come all you who avoid Me and fear Me, all you who do not know Me, come nearer to Me and you will understand that I am a God full of love, full of pity and full of mercy ...'*[2]

Fr. Jim was adamant and begged me to stop writing, if only for a few days, to see what would happen. I did so, but I prayerfully asked for a clear, specific Message from God. In reply, I received:

'I, Yahweh, am guiding you.'

Nothing more.

After three or four months of this back and forth with Fr. Jim, my husband and I became friends with Fr. Karl, who began to come to dinner with us. He gradually realized that I was not hallucinating or insane and that I had no interest in making up a story. He surprised me one day, saying that what I had received might well be a gift from God. At that point he wanted to share his ideas with Fr. Jim, the American priest.

After the two priests had discussed the matter again between themselves they advised me to go to a place in Bangladesh called

2 March 18, 1987

Diang. They explained how to reach the remote village and told me to find a Catholic hermit, Fr. Dujarrier, who lived there. He was known to have special charisms, especially that of discerning spirits. This would not be an easy trip, as first I needed to fly to Chittagong, then cross a river by canoe to reach Diang, and finally, following their instructions, find the hermit. I could not imagine going over there alone, so I shared everything with my friend Beatrice, and she offered to accompany me on the trip.

After we landed in Chittagong, we found a rickshaw driver who agreed to drive us to the river. There we spotted a canoe and asked to be taken across. Fortunately the canoeist knew the river well and made a U-turn to avoid the very strong currents. It was quite a dramatic crossing.

When we reached land, we had to hurry as night was falling, and we risked finding ourselves in the bush alone. We spotted a rickshaw and asked the man to take us to the Catholic chapel. He refused, saying that there was no road, only a path damaged by the rains. We begged him and in the end he agreed take us as far as the rickshaw could go and no further – then we must walk. We hopped on the rickshaw and off he went, but after a while on that bumpy path he brought the rickshaw to a stop and told us we had to walk the rest of the way. We walked briskly, as the sky was getting darker. After about twenty minutes we came to a halt, because right in front of us the path split in two. We couldn't believe it. 'Now what? Where do we go from here?'

We chose the left path, hoping for the best. Meanwhile, the night was closing in, and mosquitoes started to gather around us. I told Beatrice, 'If this path is not the right one, we are in real trouble.'

God was with us, however, and we were relieved to finally find ourselves facing a building surrounded by the bush, where we had been told a few priests resided. We went straight in the door and came upon a priest who, judging by the look on his face, was astonished to see us. We explained that we were looking for Fr. Dujarrier.

He kindly offered us refreshments and told us that Fr. Dujarrier did not reside there, but lived a couple of minutes away in a smaller place. He advised us to leave immediately before it was completely dark. We hurried out and walked briskly along a path through the bush again, leading to Fr. Dujarrier's dwelling. It was a poor, ramshackle place and we hurried to knock on the shabby door.

As Fr. Dujarrier opened the door, we saw he was a tall, thin man. We explained that we wanted to talk to him and we needed a place to sleep. He led us into a room with just two wooden, very simple 'beds' that looked more like platforms than beds. There were two rolled up, thin mattresses about an inch thick. We did not care, we just felt happy to have found him. He said, 'Leave your bags and come over to my dining room and have a bite with me.'

We followed him to what he called a dining room. There was no table nor chairs: simply an empty space with just a couple of straw mats on the cement floor. A local lady walked in barefoot with a tin pot and three aluminum dishes, which she placed on the straw mats in front of us. Fr. Dujarrier had taken the habit of the poor people who placed their food on the floor and ate with their hands.

After dinner, Beatrice and I spent a restless night as we noticed that there were huge spiders on the worn out curtains in our room. They had plenty to eat, as mosquitoes were buzzing around in waves. We kept our eyes fixed on them until we finally dozed off. When daylight came we noticed that in the small bathroom the dark green walls were literally covered with huge spiders. We hadn't noticed them in the dim light the night before! This was too much!

That morning I shared all my experiences with the hermit and showed him the Messages I was receiving. He studied them and after a while he looked up at me and said, 'They are from the Heart of Jesus. You have been given a gift, and you must not reject the calling of God. He wants to tell us something.'

'So it is supernatural and of divine origin?' I asked.

'Yes, it is; be faithful to your call,' he replied.

These words were enough to heal my wounds. They came on me like a healing balm.

Our hearts were lighter as we set off for the river, the first lap of our journey home. We soon felt very hungry, but there was nothing resembling a restaurant to be found. After we had crossed the river, however, we smelled food in the air. We followed the smell to a guy cooking samosas – an Indian pastry filled with spiced vegetables or meat – over a big cauldron underneath his cart. Locals sat at several tables in the small clearing, enjoying the tasty food. When they saw us two European ladies buying samosas, those sitting nearest to us vacated their seats so we could sit down. We had the table to ourselves, but as soon as Beatrice pulled out her camera, the locals crowded around us for the enjoyment of having a photo taken.

As soon as I arrived home to Dhaka, I hastened to meet up with Fr. Jim and Fr. Karl to tell them what Fr. Dujarrier had discerned. They listened attentively, and I saw that they valued the hermit's words. They both seemed relieved and from that time on changed their attitude towards me. After a time, Fr. Karl came to believe me completely and said, 'You have a gift from God, but I pity you!'

I asked him why he pitied me and he answered, 'Because if it is God who speaks to you, He will ask many heavy things of you; difficult things. He will ask you to give up most of the stuff you like which is not His, and it will not be easy for you. You will struggle a lot and you will not be left unharmed by human tongues. He will use you and you will have no rest. You will be persecuted and rejected like all the others who received the gift of prophecy and a revelation. You are lucky to live in our times and not in the past where the Inquisition had the power to burn people like you at the stake, calling them heretics and witches. But this *is* the sign that God rests on you. You will not be spared; you are not an exception; however, God will triumph through you and will be glorified. At least be happy for this is the way He treats His friends. So maybe you should look at it on the positive side that God will never leave your side. God will always be with you.'

His words could not have been more prophetic.

Then, one day as I was busy painting canvases, I sensed God was calling, repeatedly and urgently. I threw away my brush and rushed into the room where I had my notebook with the Messages. It was Jesus. He appeared as a King, majestic and mighty, the King of kings and nothing less. Smiling, He invited me to write down His Message. But what I heard next was not what I would have expected.

7

The Mission

Jesus asked, '*Tell me, which house is more important your house or My House?*'

Without hesitation I said, 'Your House, Lord.'

> '*Revive My House, embellish My House and unite My House.*'

I had no clue that the Lord's House – the Church – was *divided*. I always believed the Church was one and only nationalities changed.

I was shocked when I heard this, and almost whimpering I said, 'But how? I know nothing!'

> '*Remain nothing, for in your nothingness I shall show My power, My authority and that I AM. Die to yourself and to your ego and allow My Holy Spirit to breathe in you; allow Me to form you and mold you into what I desire you to be.*'

So in that state of stupor I asked the Lord: 'What can I do? But why did You choose me since I know nothing?'

> '*Did you not know that wretchedness attracts Me?*'

He added:

> '*Through your wretchedness I will show My mercy to the world. Come, you delight Me; children are My weakness for they allow Me to form them!*'

This encounter of daily teachings ushered me into a period of grace and bliss. It was not only like being a private pupil to Jesus under His supervision, but it was like having a spiritual honeymoon; a state of seduction. It was just the Creator and I in privacy. Every word He addressed to me was with poetry, religion and virtue. My heart was ready to do anything for Him.

So one day in that state of bliss Jesus asked me a crucial question; a question that produced an earthquake under my feet. Fear suddenly overtook me and I did not allow His words to be written when I heard them like the rest of the other conversations. I lifted my pencil in the air, refusing to write down what He had asked. My sudden distrust disappointed Him and it was obvious in His tone of Voice as He said, *'I can abide in you, despite your awesome weakness.'*

Jesus had asked:

> *'Are you willing to serve Me? Were you to serve Me, I would reveal in you nothing but Passion.'*[1]

I repeated, 'Passion?' without understanding Him, and then He said, *'Yes, Passion, will…'* but I lifted my hand at that point from the notebook, unwilling to write what came next, though I heard it all.

I realized that I had disappointed the Lord, which upset me, but I was afraid of the unknown; frightened that He might tell me to pack up and leave my house to join a Carmelite convent or something like that and become a nun.

I spent the whole night thinking about what Jesus had asked me. I remembered how I had been in the past and how He had revealed my sinful life to me so that in the future I would sin no more. Before I met the Lord I belonged to the tribe of darkness and deception, but now His Majesty had brought me into the world of Light and Truth, so what had I to fear?

So I made up my mind to go forward with blind faith and to surrender to God's Will, plunging into a spiritual world that was quite unknown to me. As I would later learn from the Scriptures: 'who can be our adversary if God is on our side?'[2]

---

1 May 23, 1987.

2 Romans 8: 31

Having thought about the situation all night long, I came back to Jesus the next day, and turned His question around,

'Do You want me to serve You?'

Immediately, I felt His joy and quivering with emotion, He said:

> *'I do! I want it very much, Vassula. Come, I will show you how and where you can serve Me ...*
>
> *'Work and serve Me as now, be as you are. I need servants who are able to serve Me where love is needed most. Work hard though, for where you are, you are among evil, unbelievers. You are in the vile depths of sin. You are going to serve your God where darkness prevails; you will have no rest. You will serve Me where every good is deformed into evil.*
>
> *'Yes, serve Me among wretchedness, among wickedness and the iniquities of the world. Serve Me among Godless people, among those that mock Me, among those that pierce My Heart. Serve Me among those that scourge Me, among My condemners. Serve Me among those that recrucify Me and spit on Me.*
>
> *'O Vassula, how I suffer! Come and console Me ... Strive and suffer with Me, share My Cross ...'*[3]

As Christ was telling me where and how I should serve Him, His emotional tempo was rising, and He was becoming more upset by the second. His grief did not escape me. Then for a whole month, Christ gave me visions of His Cross. Wherever I looked in any direction I saw a huge dark brown Cross. It was made of dark brown wood, about the size of the door. If I lifted my eyes from my plate while I was eating I would spot that Cross. If I looked through my mosquito net in bed I would see it behind the net. The vision meant my mission would be difficult, and it continued on and off for a month.

3 May 24, 1987

Then one day the Lord gave me a vision.[4] I saw three large iron bars standing near each other. This vision scared me. When the Lord sends a vision into the intellect He leaves you in no doubt as to what He means. I therefore understood what Jesus was indicating to me. These three iron bars represented the Roman Catholic Church, the Protestant Church and the Orthodox Church – the three branches of Christianity. At the same time, the Lord gave me to understand that He was going to talk to me about their individual problems.

'Aaahh, no!' I moaned. I did not want to hear about the problems of the Church! 'If they've messed it up it's their problem, not mine.' Once again I resisted hearing what God wanted to tell me.

But the vision of the three iron bars wouldn't leave me. It stayed there haunting me. So finally, without a word, I grabbed my purse, ran to my car and drove off at full speed as though I were being chased. I drove like a maniac to Dhaka's big outdoor market.

Yes! That was the best place to distract anybody. It is unbelievably busy and noisy, with hundreds of people buying and negotiating prices; beggars running after you and yanking on your clothes; sellers calling you to buy their stuff; deafening traffic of rickshaws, buses, cars, trucks and all their non-stop hooting; chickens running between your feet and herds of goats roaming freely among the people; the dirt on the ground, the stench of dust in the air mixed with the aroma of spices; the heat and the humidity. All of these created a perfect distraction, or so I had thought. But in spite of it all, the vision of the three iron bars wouldn't leave me. It remained right in front of my eyes.

Above the clamor of the market I suddenly heard a Voice right inside me calling out loudly,

> *'Pupil!'*

And then again,

> *'Get up, you have fallen! Go back and draw these three iron bars for Me.'*

---

4 June 2, 1987

I sighed, realizing it was no use running away; I had fallen into the Hands of God. I therefore drove home and did exactly what our Lord had asked me to do. Then He said,

> *'To unite you must all bend; you must all be willing to bend by softening. How could their heads [the authorities of the Churches] meet unless they all bend?'*

I understood and answered, 'I fear this work.'

> *'Leave your fears and hear Me; wait upon your God. I want to unite My Church!'* He commanded.

I felt hopeless. 'How?'

Suddenly, I heard the wildest howl coming from Satan, who shrieked in agony, 'Noooo…!' It was as if Hell's fire had grown, burning him even more than normal. The Lord ignored him and said to me,

> *'I will teach you, I will form you and I will use you, so die to yourself and allow My Holy Spirit to breathe in you. Do your best and I will do the rest; uniting My Church will be the glory of My Body. Have My peace and trust Me. Learn to walk with Me.'*

I heard the words, and I wrote them down, but I was still bewildered. After all, how could I even begin to deal with the issues in the Church? I wasn't a leader in the Church, and until recently, I didn't even go to church! And now I was going to tell them how to fix their problems? God truly has a sense of humor. But I wasn't laughing!

A few days later my Angel called me and surprised me by saying, 'You will go to Switzerland where you will sow God's seeds.'

I was compelled to write this sentence in huge, block capitals. But Switzerland was the last country where my husband would get a job assignment. His field of work was always in developing countries. So I decided to wait and see without saying anything to my husband. Sure enough, two weeks later my husband came to me and said, 'How would you like to go to Switzerland? The International Union for the Conservation of Nature and Natural Resources are asking me to work for them.'

'You won't believe it when I show you this,' I told him. Feeling jubilant, I ran off to get my Guardian Angel's Message to show it to Per. He read the prediction and saw the date of the Message. He was stunned, and so was I.

'So God is sending us to the center of Europe to start what I was called for,' I quietly thought.

Throughout the preparations for the removal the packers always worked with our garden gates open. Just as they were coming to the end of the job, dealing with the last items, a burglar took the opportunity to stroll through the wide-open entrance unnoticed and go into the house.

I had to go upstairs to the bedroom to fetch some clothes and there I saw this man just standing there. He looked petrified to see me.

'Who are you and what are you doing here?'

He did not reply and realizing he was not one of the packers, I shouted at him to get out immediately. With this he raced down the stairs while I yelled, 'There is a thief! We have a thief!'

Alerted by my shouts the packers managed to catch him, and attacked him unmercifully, one of them was beating him black and blue with a rod. At one moment I thought they would kill him, so I yelled at them to stop and let him go.

I felt a presence near me and as I turned around I saw Jesus watching. He said:

> *'You see? No one expected him to come. This is the way I will come. I will come to you as a thief. So stay alert.'*

With those words He vanished.

The following day, however, Jesus reappeared when something else happened. The gates were wide open again because they were still working, and I saw my puppy, a poodle, heading for the gates to run out in the street. I panicked and dashed as fast as I could to get to it before it was run over by the wild traffic. At that moment I heard Jesus say,

> *'Do you see how you feared for your little dog and went rushing to save it? My fears of losing souls are far greater.*

How much more are My concerns for you to save you from the dangers of death?'

That is, the danger of losing one's soul.

The packers had finally left, the house was closed up and we were about to leave Dhaka. I had kept a few things from our house thinking they might be useful for the church, and before leaving I wanted to drop them off and say farewell to the priests. I saw Fr. Jim in the church garden and carrying the gifts I went over to him. Among the items was a beautiful oil lantern, and I gave it to him personally on an impulse. As I drove off I saw him in my rear mirror walking in circles, thoughtfully looking at the lantern he held.

Perhaps my last words had unintentionally made an impression on him. As I gave him the lantern I said,

'Here, take and keep that lantern. It will be useful to give you light whenever you are in the dark.'

I had meant to imply that it would be useful for the occasions when, as sometimes happened, the electricity went down. Somehow my phrasing turned out to be symbolic for him, although that was the last I saw of him for some time.

Less than a month later, we were moving out of our house and on our way to Switzerland. It was a big change to move from Bangladesh back to Europe. And moving to Switzerland was like closing a circle, a feeling of coming home. This feeling was reinforced when we found a flat in the very road where I had lived with my parents when we first came to Lausanne.

Once I was settled back in Europe I was in a more central location to spread the Messages. And as time went on, the Messages related more and more to Unity of the Church. Jesus did not reveal everything to me all at once. My spiritual journey came in phases: every phase increasingly complex and more difficult.

One day, Jesus came with pain in His Voice to tell me that the Lance that had been thrust into His side at the crucifixion represents today the division of the Church. He said that His representatives, who are reluctant to reconcile and unite, have maimed His Body. He said that the blade of the Lance was still lying deep inside Him.

'My Body aches, right in the middle of My Heart lies the Lance's blade ...'[5]

On July 26, 1988 the Lord said:

'My Church has been wounded savagely ... and in a short time Ecclesia's Foundation will be shaken. This will be followed by the extirpation of all those who caused Her wounds and who accumulated in My Body with intention of harming It.'

It took me quite a while to understand this metaphor of the Lance. He said that He would show me the Lance's blade, which meant He would show me how the people of the Church are divided and reluctant to die to their ego and reconcile. Christ told me that during their dialogues some of them pretended they were working for unity and in fact they were not. Those who opposed the Will of Christ were the blade of the Lance, wounding the Heart of Jesus; they were the Thorns in His Mystical Body which is the Church.

From then on, Christ would ask me from time to time to pull out the Thorns and the blade from His Body and bring His Church together.

Christ made me understand that in the end the Unity of the Church will be achieved, but the question is, will it come through our voluntary cooperation, or through a Chastisement:

'Are you willing to bend with humility and love and reconcile and unite? Will you do these things with peace terms or will it be by fire?'

Christ is telling us He wants us to unite despite our differences: *unity in diversity*. Through this unity, the Body of Christ will be healed, consolidated and made whole, and Jesus' prayer to the Father will be accomplished:

'Father, may they be one in Us, as You are in Me and I am in You, so that the world may believe it was You who sent Me.'[6]

---

5 March 29, 1988

6 John 17: 21

I would need to get all the way up to the Pope and the heads of the other Churches as well, to transmit the Messages of Jesus Christ that gives them the key to unity. But I kept wondering, 'How on earth will I be able to get to them? Will they listen to me – a "nobody" who claims that God speaks to her?'

I knew that from their perspective, I would be simply too much to believe without a thorough investigation. And I knew that it wouldn't happen without a battle. Since then, there has been steady stream of attempts to destroy my name, the mission and my credibility with false accusations leveled against me, slanders too many to count, hostile verbal attacks, death threats, unending hostile confrontations from clergy – some claim I am from a UFO, an alien. Others claim I make millions of dollars; still others, that I drive around in chauffeured limos and have luxury cars. And the worst: that I am some sort of cult leader forcing people to read the Messages I receive from God. The Lord warned me on April 23, 1987:

> *'Your soul will be exposed in wickedness, in indifference, in the depths of iniquities and in the vile depths of sin of the world; as a dove flying above them you will watch the world, seeing with bitterness every action. You will be My sacrifice, you will be My target; like hunters after their game they will hunt you and pull out their weapons pursuing you; they will rate you at a high cost for whosoever could destroy you.'*

I trembled, asking in a whisper, 'Why, what will happen to me?'

Majestically, the Lord answered,

> *'I will tell you this, daughter, all will not be in vain; shadows on earth fade out and pass away; clay will always wash away with the first drops of rain, but your soul will never pass away.'*

So now it all begins; the work for Unity begins, I thought to myself. I was about to start listening to the Lord, who would be pouring out on me the disputes, their divisions and all that has gone so wrong between the Churches and made most Christians fall into apostasy.

It began to dawn on me that what I had experienced so far was only the tip of a huge iceberg. Then, just like someone opening a scroll,

God revealed to me the path of my mission, its hardships and my life in a most amazing vision.

8

The Dove

When God unrolled before my very eyes the scroll of my life it showed only codes and symbols with enigmatic signs, whose meaning I would never have understood had He not explained them to me in my intellect. He therefore preferred to show them to me in a vision.

The vision was given on January 29, 1989. I saw myself entering a large church where some sort of celebration was in progress. It was packed with people who seemed very excited. I was standing on a high, small platform looking down at the crowds. The air was filled with swirling clouds of incense. Then, in the midst of the throng I spotted a priest carrying a beautiful box. Everyone present knew that inside the box there was a special Dove, and I realized later that it represented the Holy Spirit. The Priest, who represented Christ, was supposed to open the box and allow the Dove to fly around us giving us great joy! He did not want to keep us waiting so he opened the box and out came the Dove.

When the people saw the Dove flying above them, they felt exhilarated with joy and when the Dove flew lower, coming close to them, they all exclaimed great 'ahhh's! Their enthusiasm and excitement filled the church. For a time the Dove continued to fly around in circles. I noticed that quite often the Dove approached me. We all lifted our arms high in the air, hoping to attract the Dove to come to perch on our hands. We knew that the Dove in the end would choose one of us, and we also knew that the person chosen would be greatly privileged.

While the Dove was circling above us I felt convinced in my heart that we knew each other and were somehow friends. As one would say, 'We connected.' The Dove was a sky-blue color – not white, and later on I learned that the color blue represents 'the Divine'. I saw the Dove heading towards me, and in my heart I knew It was going to rest on me, for I sensed this communication between us. And as the Dove finally came to rest on my fingertips, I not only felt a great familiarity towards It, I also sensed that a deep and intimate love existed between us.

All eyes turned in my direction. Some people were surprised by the Dove's choice; others had seriously hoped that the Dove would fly to them; others were delighted that It had finally made Its choice. After a few moments the Dove flew off and then, having flown around the church, It circled once more and flew towards me again, coming to rest on my fingertips. This time the Dove allowed me to hold It in my hands and I, melting with joy, very carefully and with tenderness lifted It and pressed It lovingly to my left cheek near my ear. I listened to Its quick heartbeats, as Its heart was throbbing loudly.

Then suddenly I found myself alone – walking on a path. All along the side of this path were unknown little animals, similar to squirrels. They were mercilessly swallowing each other. In front of me on the path I saw a large rat gripping a small animal in its mouth scurrying menacingly towards me, trying to frighten me. I did not fear, and to show the rat that I was 'in control and master' I hastened my step towards it. It sensed immediately that I was going to confront it and so, frightened, it turned aside and ran to attack a squirrel-like animal from behind, swallowing it whole with an ugly gurgling sound. Then, a short distance away, I saw a snake stretched from one side of the path to the other, blocking my way. I thanked God for letting me see it, because it was as transparent as cellophane. That made it difficult to spot, and had I stepped on the snake it would have bitten me. I was not frightened; I had made up my mind to continue walking and just step over it.

When I had passed it, I heard a slight noise close behind me. Another snake, slithering rapidly, came to catch up with me. It was entirely different from the first one and I knew this one was aggressive and ready to attack – no matter what. It too was transparent, with just a small, dark, zigzag design on its back. It must have been nine feet long and was as thin as a finger. I felt trapped, but immediately something wonderful happened: God came to my rescue and levitated me high above the ground. Yet, I was still anxious for I sensed its evil intentions, and thought that it might rear up to reach me. At that moment my Heavenly Father swiftly lifted me forward, as though blown with the wind, passing me safely above the snakes, and placing me on the ground, next to a friend of mine.

My friend and I were now standing at the end of the path, facing a wall. We were not afraid, but I heard something and turned my head slightly to the right where I saw the first snake that had blocked the path. I understood it was searching for food, and as of yet it didn't see us. My friend had not seen the snake so I whispered, 'Don't move; remain still.' I didn't tell her about the snake in case she reacted and drew its attention. Then I saw the long thin snake arrive and slither next to the first one. Swiftly and with great ferocity the first snake attacked the thin one, giving it no chance to defend itself, and swallowed it with a repulsive gurgling sound. I felt relieved and secure, knowing that the snake was now content and would only want to sleep, thus leaving us in peace and out of danger. Then the vision ended.

I did not fully understand this vision, but over time, God began to reveal to me what everything meant. The Dove symbolically represented the Holy Spirit. When the Dove landed on my hands, this represented that God chose me to give me His Messages for our generation: a special mission to carry out in life.

The rat, and the snakes, were representing that on the path of my mission I would encounter difficulties, controversy, obstacles, and people who would try and strike me in a subtle way without revealing themselves. Their acts would be done hypocritically and under cover to avoid detection, so that no one discovers who the predators really are. This was the reason I was shown snakes as transparent as cellophane, '*a replica of the Pharisees*'[1] as Christ put it one day.

This vision was given to me just before I began to publicly witness for the first time ever – to tell others – about the Messages I had been receiving. How this witnessing came about was quite interesting.

1 September 1, 1987

At this point, I was living in Switzerland. I was at a gathering one day, just about to leave, when an elderly lady with a hump who had previously been a nun approached me and asked in a sweet and frail voice, 'Are you Vassula of Pully, who receives Messages from Christ and from Our Lady?' She had heard about me through some friends.

Surprised, I answered, 'Yes, that's me ...'

She went on, 'Oh, would you mind me bringing some friends of mine over to your house so that we can hear your story?' I said that would be fine and we fixed a date.

When the doorbell rang that day, I opened the door to find about thirty people standing there! Our apartment was tiny and they filled the sitting room, spilling out into the hall, all the way to the kitchen. I was overwhelmed with joy! I started to tell my story and explained how it all began, first with my Angel, then with God the Father, then with Jesus and the Virgin Mary. They all listened attentively in silence, nodding now and then, showing their understanding and their approval.

A lady sitting opposite me introduced herself. She organized pilgrimages to important sites where holy apparitions had taken place, especially recent ones. At the end of my talk she immediately spoke out, obviously excited. With a twinkle in her eye she said, 'That *is* a beautiful testimony and the Message sounds *so* important ...' Everyone nodded in agreement. Together they talked about finding a place where I could share even more of the Messages of our Lord.

It was later decided that we'd have this larger meeting at the Parish Hall of a local church. They had spoken to the priest and had received his permission, and they said they would do the work of promoting the event.

About a month before that first public meeting, I saw our Lord standing nearby while I was in my kitchen. He looked at me as I passed close to Him at the kitchen door, and murmured, '*I am sending you out now as a sheep among wolves ...*' Then He disappeared. I remembered my vision of the Dove and I took Jesus' words as a warning. This was a confirmation that I would not have it easy ...

I cannot say that I had not been warned several times by God that the apostolate would bear severe trials.

As the days approached for my first witnessing in public, a temptation entered me. I began to ask myself, 'Have I lost my freedom?' I realized my old, carefree life was fading away. I was abandoning certain friends and giving up my favorite pastimes, tennis and painting. I was losing interest in going to parties and playing bridge. I was losing interest in everything that took my mind away from God. I used to mock people like this, but lo and behold was I starting to resemble them? Was I becoming a bigot, a 'holier than thou' person, as I used to think they were? Was I losing my freedom and being forced to live a good life, instead of just doing whatever I wanted?

Since I knew no one can hide their thoughts from God, I brought the subject up to our Lord.

I told Him that in the beginning, before He approached me, my life had been worldly but joyful and peaceful. I had no cares or worries. However, I started to feel that the Word of God began to weigh heavily on me – it was this responsibility that weighed on me, especially when God used to tell me now and then: '*I am entrusting you with My Message.*'

'Your Word, my God, is so *heavy!!* Where is my freedom now?'

Our Lord replied as a patient Father, and said,

> *'I, the Lord, will let you know what freedom is. Write: freedom is when your soul detaches itself from earthly solicitudes and flies towards Me, to Me. I, God, came and liberated you; you are free now. When you were attached to the world, Vassula, you were a prisoner of all its temptations, but your soul now like a dove has been freed; you were caged beloved; caged; let your soul fly out freely, let it feel this freedom I have given to all of My souls, but how many of them refuse this grace I offered. Do not let yourself be caught again, tied and caged, I have liberated you.*[2]

It would take time, but I was learning; I was learning that where the Spirit of the Lord is, *there* is true freedom. I also learned that when God speaks He doesn't speak in dark corners but reveals the

2 April 23, 1987

whole truth in full light and with transparency. He is so ready and with ineffable longing, to provide whatever one asks from Him. He gives much more than we ask! This is how generous He is. I knew that I did not know how to love God, not the way He wanted, which is unconditional and without limit.

The day of my first public meeting finally arrived. I had never spoken on a platform before and doing so terrified me. When I got to the church hall, close to three hundred people were there! When I saw them all, I panicked. I walked over to the church next door and knelt in front of a huge crucifix, lamenting to Jesus, 'Lord, what am I to say? Look what You've put me into now. How am I to speak? What shall I say? I've never spoken or witnessed before ...' I sighed. 'I need Your help.' And again, 'Lord, see what a situation You have put me in. I did not ask for this, as You know ... If You do not help me, not only will I embarrass myself but I will embarrass You, as well! We don't want that to happen! Take this fear and insecurity away from me; touch my lips and give me speech. I need You to encourage me, and place the right words in my mouth. I need Your Holy Spirit of Grace to be able to glorify You and not ridicule You ...'

Then I remembered how many times He had told me,

> *'Do not worry, I will guide you, and you will not fail Me ...*
> *where you lack I will fill ... I will place My Words on your lips,*
> *I will enrich your speech; your speech will be My speech ...'*

Then the Lord answered and said as a command,

> *'The time has come to glorify Me, go!'*

I got up and went straight to the parish hall. As I walked in, I had only one thought in my head, and that was to do my best to glorify God. Christ had also told me, as He tells all of us, *'Do your best and I shall do the rest ...'*

Suddenly I no longer felt my feet walking. I felt myself gliding forward, as if in a dream, in slow motion. Then I felt an incredible peace filling me, as a warm liquid pouring through the top of my head all the way down to my feet, filling every part of my body. It felt like Someone breathing His warm breath into me giving me total reassurance; a majestic authority that was not mine and a deep peace in my soul. I knew that God was pouring into me His Holy Spirit of Grace. I physically felt this act.

I opened my mouth and the words poured out. It was like listening to myself speak, and realizing it was not I who was speaking. It was guided, as I would have been incapable of giving it on my own. Many people were cut to the heart, and after my talk, my cousin said, 'Vassula, I have never seen you like this before! You were like a fish in water. You spoke as though you had preached all your life!' She knew that I had never studied any catechism or theology or spoken in public before.

After this point, I was asked to give my testimony regularly. We created a program once a month in Switzerland, which included prayer meetings. These prayer meetings soon became a source of joy and conversion for many people. The crowds steadily became larger, coming close to two thousand. People came to Switzerland by the busload from the neighboring countries of Germany, Italy, and France. The Lord called everyone! They brought their families, their friends; they brought the sick, the possessed, and many healings were performed. Jesus was not afraid to dispense His graces to everyone. A mere smile to Him and He would forgive and forget; a sigh of regret and reconsideration and all Heaven would rejoice and feast! Here are His own words:

> *'Come! You who err still in this wilderness saying: "I have sought my Redeemer but have not found Him." Find Me My beloved in purity of heart, by loving Me without self-interest. Find Me in holiness, in the abandonment I desire of you. Find Me by observing My Commandments; find Me by replacing evil with love; find Me in simplicity of heart. Sin no more. Cease in doing evil; learn to do good; search for justice; help the oppressed. Let this wilderness and this aridity exult! Let your tepidity inflame into an ardent flame. Relinquish your apathy and replace it by fervor. Do all these things so that you may be able to say: "I have sought my Redeemer and I have found Him. He was near me all the time, but in my darkness I failed to see Him. O Glory be to God! Blessed be our Lord!*

> *How could I have been so blind?" I shall then remind you to keep and treasure My principles so that you may live.'*[3]

When my friends, astounded by the speed at which the Messages were circulating around the world, asked me how I felt, I replied,

'No one should dare venture to say, "What has God done for us?" In God's sight the whole world is like a grain of dust that tips the scales, like a drop of morning dew falling on the ground. Yet God is merciful to all, because He can do all things and overlooks men's sins so long as they repent.'

I could sense the movement above in Heaven. God was giving generously, pouring out graces. He said that no one should fear Him unless they rebelled against Him. He spoke to all of us, no matter what our religion or background. Priests and nuns started to join with us to pray and listen to the Messages. We all felt Him in our hearts!

I remind people that God is not a God of the past but of the present. God has not packed His bags and left us to go on a holiday. He is the Living God, a Father concerned for each one of us; meek and tender. Christ has indeed risen: it is not a myth.

After a few months, my name started to make a lot of noise in Switzerland and from there it spread to other countries. The Messages of our Lord – which were now being copied and distributed at my witnessing meetings – started to have an effect, just as God and my Angel had foretold. They were spreading like wildfire. Many people with weak faith became stronger, and those without faith received and discovered Jesus Christ. People ran to confession, and received Holy Communion again. Those who never prayed started to pray fervently. Those who never read the Scriptures plunged into the Holy Bible, reading it from the start. Those who had abandoned their Church for this or that reason returned to their Churches, rediscovering the Sacraments and rediscovering God Almighty.

God was throwing open the doors of His Celestial Reserves, allowing people who were spiritually starved to taste and eat this 'celestial manna' to renew and heal them. Wherever He found the

---

3 August 9, 1989

spiritually dead, without hesitation He would resurrect them, so long as their hearts were open to His grace. He was ready to forgive and forget.

> *'And we, with our unveiled faces reflecting like mirrors the brightness of the Lord, all grew brighter and brighter as we were turned into the image that we reflect; this is the work of the Lord who is Spirit.'*[4]

As the word continued to spread, it eventually reached the ears of the Bishop of Fribourg. He received letters telling him about the large prayer meetings; how wonderful they were, and asking him to meet me. Before agreeing, however, the Bishop found it prudent to ask a priest, a theologian, who was of English origin, to investigate the matter and to study the contents of the Messages. The theologian contacted me and, accompanied by another priest, we met in my home. At one point during our conversation he suddenly stopped talking. His eyes were fixed on me and he stared hard. His companion asked him, 'Are you seeing something?' He answered, 'I am seeing the Face of Christ on her face. He is wearing His crown of thorns and is smiling sadly at me.'

This phenomenon (which I explain in later chapters) was a sign that Jesus gave, and I personally had no control over it. It has happened many times. The priest asked me, 'Why is Christ showing Himself to me? And why is He sad?' I told him that I honestly did not know. When he left he took photocopies of my notebooks with him to study, as he had promised the Bishop.

After a few days he wrote to me, saying that he had found nothing in any of the Messages that went against the Catholic faith and that all he had read conformed to the Scriptures and Catholic tradition. He said that he found humility and love in the writings.

He went on to say that he had met by chance his Bishop, who asked how his investigations were going. He had replied that in his opinion the contents of the writings appeared to be of Divine origin. The Bishop seemed taken aback, not expecting such an answer,

4 2 Corinthians 3: 18

and apparently not very happy with the news. Despite this positive investigation and good report, the Bishop turned against me and persecuted our work in Switzerland.

Rumors went around that I was lacking in humility, that I believed myself to be a theologian and that in my own way I was trying to create a parallel Church. This negative current reached all the way to the Vatican and it did us a great deal of harm. God's warning resounded again in my ears:

> *'You will be My sacrifice, you will be My target; like hunters after their game they will hunt you and pull out their weapons pursuing you; they will rate you at a high cost for whosoever could destroy you.'*[5]

At that time I met the Metropolitan of the Greek Orthodox Church of Geneva, who actually approached me and was eager to get to know me. He happened to come over to visit the Orthodox Church of Lausanne, where I lived, to celebrate the Liturgy, and when he saw me, with a broad smile he invited me to go to his office to see him. He had been asked to interview me by others who had met me.

I went to see him, and we sat and talked and I told him my story in brief. He appeared to be very pleasant and polite. Even though I knew he had a problem believing me, I asked permission to hold ecumenical prayer meetings, bringing together members of the Greek Orthodox Church with our brothers the Catholics and Protestants. I told him that one of the most important parts of the mission was to bring the Churches together. I was delighted when he said that he had no objections at all.

Unfortunately our good relationship did not last, as the Bishop of Fribourg was working to shut down our prayer meetings altogether. Priests who had been attending these meetings could not understand the Bishop's decision, but they were obliged to accept his authority.

But the Messages continued to spread anyway. One night, the Lord gave me a vision. I saw a huge snake rather like a gigantic anaconda. In fact it was even bigger, its head larger than that of a big dog. I was

---

5 April 23, 1987

frightened beyond imagination because the snake intertwined with me. The snake's head came closer and I saw its fangs. It approached my right hand and with its mouth it took hold of three of my fingers, the very fingers used by Orthodox Christians to cross themselves. The snake grasped the fingers tightly sucking them with force until they hurt so much that the pain woke me up. The pain was real, as it continued for a while.

Just a day after that nightmare, I was due to speak at a meeting organized by the Geneva prayer group. It was during Unity Week, January 18–25, and our meeting was arranged for early afternoon. On the same day the Metropolitan was holding a meeting in his church, but later in the afternoon, after my event. We had purposely scheduled our meeting so as not to overlap with his. When the Metropolitan learned that two thousand people had attended my meeting, while only a small crowd attended his, he was very annoyed. He accused me of trying to compete with him, saying that I had taken people away from him and was creating a parallel Church. He even accused me of working against the Church.

The next day, my cousin called me and said, 'Vassula, there are rumors going around among the Greek people saying that you will be excommunicated. Be careful; don't do anything for a while. Keep a low profile for a time.'

I asked her, 'On what basis would they excommunicate me?'

'We don't know what their arguments will be, but for sure they don't like the popularity of your meetings.'

'What's wrong with having prayer meetings? Are they trying to stop people from gathering to pray?'

A few days later I received a call from Beatrice, the friend who followed me to Diang in Bangladesh, who had come to Switzerland as well and taken a job in the World Council of Churches in Geneva. She told me, 'A few theologians from here have left to visit the Ecumenical Patriarch of Constantinople for discussions. They will also meet with several of the Roman Curia from the Vatican. Do you remember, I once told you of an Orthodox priest here who believes in your Messages? Well, his wife has been reading the Messages and also believes. She is a theologian and is very alarmed because some of the others working here want to hurt you. On the way to Constantinople an Orthodox priest showed her the agenda to be discussed at the Patriarchate, and said, "Look, about this Vassula, the one who plays the theologian, they will discuss the matter with the Patriarch to excommunicate our so-called theologian."'

I received the news and asked God: 'If You want it that way, let it be so, but if you don't agree, do not let it happen ...' I entrusted myself entirely to His Will. I knew the impact the Messages were already having, and how badly the devil wanted to stop me, and wanted to create division between me and the Church leaders, in order to limit my reach.

My heart suddenly filled with joy. I slammed down the receiver and gave a leap in the air and hopped around, dancing with joy, laughing and saying: 'How wonderful to be feared by Satan! That means that what I am carrying is dreadful for Satan, a real threat against him. Wow! How wonderful to be his dangerous enemy and work for God! How wonderful to be God's instrument to fight the devil who wants to destroy the Church! Rejoice!'

The nightmare of the snake had come true. The huge snake wanted to destroy the three fingers I use to cross myself – in other words to excommunicate me.

But when the meeting took place in Constantinople, it was as though nothing had happened. They returned without a statement and the whole thing died out.

Some of the Greek Orthodox clergy nonetheless would approach me and say, 'You have a family don't you? So go, my good woman, and serve your husband and your family; stick to your household chores and the kitchen; leave these Church affairs to us.'

'On Judgment Day,' I would respond, 'you will not be in my shoes to answer for me if I were to listen to you. The Lord will ask *me* to account for not having obeyed Him and for not having done the things He communicated and commanded me to do! Have you seen the widespread loss of faith, and the people leaving the Churches? Is that not enough of a sign for you? His Vineyard has been neglected and has dried out, and for this reason, Christ, to show His Authority and His Power is calling the nobodies like me to form them and use them as His instruments to Christianize a de-Christianized society.

Christ has stepped down from His icons to reform His Church and to revive it. *He* is the One who waters His Vineyard again; *He* is the One and only that will bring the Churches to reconcile with one another and bring peace to this world. Christ is known to take away the sight of those who claim they see and give sight to those who did not see!'

Then they would say, 'If you are sent by God, prove your humility by hiding yourself and all those sayings, stop parading yourself and your sayings around the world …'

Years later, the Lord advised me how to answer these people in this way:

> *'To these people answer the following: "I am not going to be like the wicked servant who hid his talent and then was condemned for having done nothing; on the contrary, I will multiply my talent and give glory to the One who entrusted it to me. I will pass on, not only to this generation this prodigious wonder, but the angels will carry the Words of God and will continue spreading them like a rain of seeds thrown from above to all future generations to renew God's creation and embellish the Church; to sweeten the mouths of His children and open their mouths to praise Him; to open their eyes and enable them to examine their hearts; I am sealed by our Lord's Divine Name all over me and I do not fear. I am His Loud Book declaring the same Truths our Lord has passed on to us, so nothing is new. I have nothing new that is of my own, brothers, but all that is said to me comes from Divine Knowledge and from the Mouth of the Triune God." This is what you are to tell them in My Name.'*[6]

The Lord had said in the past,[7]

> *'Vassula, you shall face severe trials … when I see how so many of My sacerdotal souls deny My Signs and My Works and how they treat those to whom I have given My graces to remind the world I am among you, I grieve … they deny My Works, thus making deserts instead of making the land fertile!'*

6 August 7, 2002

7 July 7, 1987

Seeing how upset our Lord was with them, I dared to respond and then, to justify them I said:

'Lord, if they deny Your Works, there must be reasons!'

He answered,

> *'Spiritually they are dead. They are deserts themselves, and when they spot a flower in that great wilderness they made, they rush to it and trample it, destroying it.'*

'Why?'

> *'Why? It is a misfit in their wilderness; they make sure that their desert stays arid! I find no holiness in them, none! What have they to offer Me?'*

I managed to say, 'Protection Lord, protection so that Your Word is not distorted.'

Immediately He said,

> *'No, they are not protecting Me; they are denying Me as God. They deny My Infinite Wealth, they deny My Omnipotence, they are comparing themselves to Me. Do you know what they are doing? They are promoting paganism, they are multiplying My scourgers; they are increasing spiritual deafness; they are not defending Me, they are deriding Me! I have willed, in spite of their denials, to help them so that in their turn they would help and feed My lambs.'*

I felt sad for God … He replied,

> *'Beloved, grieve for the world and what it has become …'*

This is not to say that all clergy or Church leaders are bad. There are many who are good, and many who are doing the Lord's Will. In fact, God compares the shepherds in some Messages to Cain and Abel. Cain was not pleasing to God for he was not doing God's Will but Abel was.

I was beginning to live the vision of the Dove, traversing the difficult and dangerous path I had seen in the vision.

9

Supernatural

All working of grace is supernatural. All these supernatural and mystical experiences that have occurred to me can be attributed to God. God uses these supernatural communications, favors, and gifts without any activity on my part. These visions, spiritual dreams, miracles, perfumes, and enlightenments have been given abundantly *for His Glory* and for our benefit and the benefit of the Church.

God will explain:

> *'I want to let you know how I work; have you not heard that I speak by dreams, visions and signs? I speak first in one way, then in another until I am heard.'*[1]

However, not all dreams are Messages from God – only spiritual dreams, or what is known as the 'sleep language of God'. In the Bible, God names His Prophet: 'dreamer of dreams'.[2] The virtue of a dream is that in one fast-moving reel God can speak with minimum conscious interference. In my case, I have had many spiritual dreams which I sometimes call 'visions'.

Before I continue to give more explanations on this subject, I would like to share my experiences and conversations with God, as this alone *is* supernatural. I will share my fears, my hesitations and my weakness, and how exactly through these, God shows His Powerful Hand and His great love.

---

1 My Angel Daniel, January 19, 1987

2 Deuteronomy 13: 1

One day in September 1987, the year I moved to Switzerland, I was getting frustrated that I was not yet given opportunities to pass on and share the Messages of God. He was sort of 'pushing' me to speak about them and yet, in His absolute wisdom He was not giving me an open door, because He had His own time. I lost my patience and said to Jesus: 'You are asking me to make Your Message known, but I am not doing much! For the time being I am only making photocopies and giving them to a few relatives and friends who want to read them.' Jesus replied calmly,

> *'You will do a lot more than photocopies.'*

For days I kept asking God to give me the reasons why He chose me, a 'professional sinner,' asking Him to take, instead of me, a holy nun and give her these Messages.

He listened patiently, allowing me to blabber on and on, then simply said,

> *'No ... No! I want <u>you</u>. You are the prototype of your generation.'*

I knew that this was not exactly a compliment. Was I really portraying what we have become today?

I was not ready for higher experiences; God, however, was doing a lot for my soul, raising my mind to taste the higher levels of Heaven and the glory surrounding Him. He said,[3]

> *'Come and lean on Me; the time has not yet come. In the meantime be watchful and stay awake.'*

There is the risk of deviating when the mind does not remain vigilant. God wanted to remind me of the past, so that I could clearly understand the difference. He explained it in this way,

> *'I was pleased that although you seemed to have forgotten Me, you heard My voice. I wanted you to love Me. I wanted you to*

3 My Angel Daniel, December 2, 1986

understand how much I love you. Learn that I, God, always reach My goals.'

His words consoled me and I felt relieved. He continued and said,

'When I appeared the first time to you, I held you so that you lifted your head and looked at the One who was in front of you. When you lifted your head, I looked into your eyes and saw how unloved you felt.'

That is, unloved by God. Many of us still believe that because of our sinfulness and our wretchedness, God's love diminishes. Yes, I had not known or understood that God could love someone like me who never prayed or practiced her faith, lived loaded with sin and rebelled against His Law. I always thought that He loved those who loved Him, worshipped Him and were leading a holy life. Most people think the way I did, imagining that we have to be perfect in God's eyes to be loved by Him. I remember when God said in one of His Messages,[4] *'Do not wait to become a saint to offer Me your love, come as you are!'* In fact, because He reads our hearts, He knew of my guilt and of my wickedness and He pitied me. It is the sin He hates.

Several times God revealed to me how frail we are and how easy it is for us to stray away from His Light and dwell in perpetual darkness. We do it without even noticing. Here I was, newly drawn to God and in spite of the weight of grace I was receiving, I was still confused, frail, and insecure.

I dared to blurt out to the Lord,

'All those who received Your calls were rejected, ridiculed and declared mad! Some were burned at the stake. In our modern society I'll be scorned! Some might even go as far as to say that I'm possessed.'

God patiently replied,[5]

'Let them approach you those that want to laugh at you, little would they know how grave their accusations would be for they would be laughing on My given Words. I will deal

4 August 19, 1988

5 My Angel Daniel, December 2, 1986

> *with these later on. Have faith in Me. I will call you again to whisper in your ear preaching. I will fill up your mouth with My Words. I, Yahweh am your Strength.'*

Then to reassure me, the Lord emphasized the following: *'I will give you enough strength to enable you to overlook your oppressors, who will be many, My child.'*

I whimpered, for I noticed how God's Voice had suddenly dropped and turned grave and very sad. He sounded like a father who was obliged to sacrifice one of his beloved sons to go off to war, knowing that he will be tortured and might not even return alive. He continued:

> *'But I will cover you with My shield. No one will be able to harm you.'*

Encouraged by these words, I thought, my God and All, with what ingenuity Your affection and Your paternal love stretches out to reach and care for Your creatures who lie in oblivion and in the valley of death as a consequence of their apostasy.

Within me I knew that God was preparing me not only to meet greater trials but also to meet the Enemy: all that can make one's heart bleed with pain. I began to feel the effects of that Message, and once more my heart began to be agitated. I feared being mocked by people. My humanity was taking over my spirit once more. I argued:

'My Lord and King, although you sent me one of the noblest Princes from your celestial Court to guide me to You, one of the highest ranked Princes and Archangels to entice my soul and follow You, I feel totally unfit for the task. I am most despicable, with stains on my soul and with defects. How will You triumph through such misery? Will You not cheapen Your Scepter? We are in 1987! Some people will not accept this revelation. "We have the Holy Bible to study", they will say!'

Then God replied,[6]

> *'These ecclesiastical messages are a reminder, for in My Heart was a day of mercy. The hour of My saving help is here, after all am I not Father? Am I not the saving of My seeds? … I*

6 My Angel Daniel, January 1, 1987

want to remind you that My Word is meant to be read. My Word is blessed. I am the Almighty God and am free to step out whenever I please. Why did you think, daughter, that I will make any difference because you are in 1987? Your era makes no difference to Me. Listen, for Me a thousand years is yesterday. My door will always remain open ...'

I whimpered,

'Jesus told us once that a prophet is never accepted in his own homeland. Many will not accept me as Your bearer. Most of Your messengers were treated as fools, or told they were possessed; they were *slain*!'

'Live in peace, daughter, lean on Me. I, God, will be your Strength. With Me you need not fear. I will help you ...'

Here I was, receiving the words of God, yet in spite of all the good things I had experienced, I felt worried and imprisoned in my bones. After such an incredible union with God, I still lacked confidence.

I was being called daily, filling notebooks with divine teachings dictated by our Lord with great delight, not knowing where this would lead me. I was intertwined with the natural and the supernatural. At the same time He was giving me continual visions and prophecies for our times and yet I was not giving Him the right responses.

During these days of weakness, God gave me a spiritual dream to encourage me. In it, I saw myself on a rough road. As I went along, I tripped and fell. I lifted up my eyes and saw the bare feet of Jesus. He bent down and pulled me to my feet. I turned around and saw a familiar figure – a monk. He spoke to me in Italian, gesturing with his hands. Although I had never met him before and only knew of him by reputation, I recognized the monk as Saint Padre Pio, who had lived in Italy in the 1900s and had borne the 'stigmata', the wounds of Christ, in his hands and feet. Padre Pio made me understand that I should not give up following the path God had set for me and he seemed quite upset that I had such doubts. Near him, but closer to me, I saw St Francis of Assisi, and next to him a very tall ladder that led up to Heaven. As I looked up, I saw far above me at the top of the ladder the silhouettes of many Saints gesturing for me to climb up. I realized that I was at the very bottom and had not even put my foot on the first step of the ladder. I had not yet begun my ascent.

The day after I had this dream, I answered a call from Heaven, and it turned out to be Saint Pio himself. He encouraged me saying, '*Io sono con te*,' meaning, 'I am with you.' I was amazed. I asked Jesus, 'Is he with you?' He replied, '*Yes, he is with Me, Vassula, and beatified by Me …*'[7]

God will give us supernatural dreams like this, and other supernatural signs, to reassure us of His presence. I have learned from my experiences to know the difference between God's supernatural activities as opposed to natural or preternatural activity. Our soul can easily see the natural, for it deals with the physical world. For example, we may be reminded of God's transcendent beauty while looking at the beautiful scenery of nature.

The preternatural is the action that goes beyond the structure of the nature, of material universe. The fruit of the action of an angelic or demonic nature is said to be preternatural.

God can go further than that – He can send spiritual graces of repentance, praise, and thanksgiving to the deepest depths of one's soul, causing radical changes in seconds. He can touch our heart, convert us and bring us to a life of prayer. This can only come from grace.

There are different ways I enter into supernatural communications with God. The main way is when He calls me. I feel His call – whether I hear His Voice, or just feel it – and I immediately know He's asking me to listen to Him. This way of communication is called locution. I get a bit anxious with whatever I'm doing in the material world. I want to finish it quickly so I can get myself free to be in the spiritual world. God is like a magnet that draws me in, and once connected, I don't want to let go.

My soul is lifted and sated with delight when in His Lordly style He invites me to write His Message. As I pick up my pencil, I feel a tingling in my arm, like electricity, and I start to hear His Message. As I hear it, I write it. He dictates to me, and I write what He says,

7 September 27, 1987

verbatim. When He opens His Mouth to speak, a ray of Light streams out and covers me. Then, in a melodious Voice, He will say,

'Do you still want to be with Me in this way and write?'

reminding me of our liberty to choose. Then I, trembling and faint, totally defeated by His gaze on me, lose all memory of the world in front of this wondrous sight. His transcendent Light can shine on anyone who is willing to offer Him their will. Yes, anyone, without exception.

While receiving the Message I do not fall into a trance, which is what happens to people who are dealing with the occult or 'automatic' writing. It's also different from what some have experienced, called 'ecstasies', when they see the supernatural world. When a person is 'in ecstasy', as some of the Saints have described, they are totally removed. You could go up to them and poke them and they won't feel anything. They're completely in the spiritual world.

I am asked by many people, especially the clergy, 'Why does the Lord choose to transform your own handwriting, even seizing your hand?' I answer truthfully, 'I really don't know.'

But, one day I myself put this same question to the Lord and His reply made me smile. He simply said, *'I like it this way.'*[8]

Right, then I have nothing to add.

However, since many people are intrigued about the change of writing I would like to mention that this is not automatic writing. Fr. Curty of France, a renowned and powerful exorcist as well as a graphologist, studied my case, as did other graphologists. Indeed they knew from their experience in that field that people using automatic writing suffered certain consequences and eventually risk becoming possessed.

They found that the handwriting of the Messages has nothing to do with automatic writing. Fr. Curty described many groundbreaking differences between the way I write and automatic writing. He named the handwriting of the Messages 'hieratic writing' which means sacred writing. I have come to know that among other well-known

8 November 7, 1989

mystics, St Teresa of Avila experienced raptures of the body or at times just part of her body. I believe that what I experience in my hand is a mitigated form of rapture, and trust that the Lord has His own purposes for this. As I said, the Lord teaches in a simple way, adapting Himself to the individual.

When I'm conversing with God in the spiritual world, I still know what's going on around me in the material world. I'm present in both the material world *and* the supernatural world at the same time.

One time in Bangladesh when I was having a locution and writing down the Message, my housekeeper came in yelling about something, a telegram I needed to sign for. It was such a disruption in the middle of my communication with Jesus that I yelled back at the person to 'Get out!' But then Jesus, being so kind, softly reprimanded me. *'Be calm,'* He said. It was so sweetly said that it was like a cold shower extinguishing my spark. And I understood again how meek and humble He is.

At other times, I can begin this communication with God by simply going into prayer. I will begin to pray, just as anyone else does, and I will write down my thoughts to Him. But as I do that, He will directly answer me, and I will begin to write the words He is saying to me. This is one unique aspect of the gift God has given me. He has told me:

> *'Unlike others who receive My Word as a gift and whom I visit when I wish, I have given you a unique gift, this one of calling Me at any time you wish. See? I have given you this special privilege in proportion to the task I have entrusted you with and in proportion to My burden on you. See, how I measured everything when I planned this? Not that you were qualified in yourself for this most noble task of reviving and uniting My House; all your qualifications come from My bounty, they come from Me. I have made you the vessel that carries this immense treasure, frail but clear, that such an overwhelming Power does not come from you but from Me, your God.'*[9]

9 August 29, 1998

Regardless of how long one of these encounters lasts, it always comes to an end eventually. And when it does, it is an anti-climax; I would even say it's painful. Imagine being in a bright, splendid and majestic court, and then abruptly being pulled down into soot and darkness. As it happens, I look around me, and as God once said, '*still dripping with Heavenly dew*'[10] I see the physical world with a heightened awareness, and how trivial things are. Things that I thought important and significant on earth are nothing compared to God's splendor.

Once I was with a good friend of mine, and God called me. He lifted my soul to His Heavenly Court while giving me a Message. When the Message was completed my friend came over to me and gave me a hug. In spite of being close friends, I found her touch unbearable at that moment, as I always do at such times. Her embrace didn't hurt me from the outside, but within my soul I had a painful feeling of discomfort.

Some people ask me how I 'know' who is speaking to me when I am receiving Messages. I have no problem knowing whether it is the Father, Jesus Christ, the Virgin Mary, or an Angel communicating with me because a light of understanding and knowledge is given into my intellect.

God adapts Himself to us in a very delicate manner. The revelations God has given me are simple, almost human, so to speak. This is so that they do not shock us. God manifests Himself through the visions by taking the form of a Man. This is in order to avoid my fearing Him when He approaches, and to ensure that the Divine and the human, the supernatural and the natural, are intertwined. This is what Jesus said in a Message:

> *'I wish to make it known to you that I do approach in a supernatural way giving My Messages; do not forget that I am God of Mercy and in spite of your wretchedness and the indifference you had towards Me, I love you; I gave you this charism so that you learn directly from My lips; Vassula, resting in your heart feels good.'*[11]

---

10 November 30, 1998

11 March 8, 1987

Someone once claimed that there was nothing supernatural about my experiences and that they must be just my own private meditations. I said to that person, 'What do you consider to be proof that something is supernatural?' I did not get an answer.

However, I knew the answer. Supernatural is the action which goes beyond any created nature. This form of activity belongs only to God. The supernatural is a *spontaneous* conversion of the heart that leads to repentance. It is when the Holy Spirit touches our hearts and brings us to a life of prayer. It is when we give our entire life to Christ. It is when God, through His grace plants a fire within us and turns us into living torches ready in our turn to set ablaze the whole world and bring it to compunction. Only God's supernatural action can lift a soul to praise and worship Him all day long. Those things are not natural – they are the fruits of supernatural grace.

Some of my old friends who knew nothing about God, once said, 'Maybe all this comes from your mind. You know, some sort of ESP (extrasensory perception) or your subconscious at work – you know how the subconscious can play tricks.'

'I'm sorry,' I tell them, 'my subconscious was blank in regards to spiritual matters. So this experience of God cannot come from a blank sheet.'

'Maybe in your inner self you wanted to become a nun, and this is the result of your suppressed desire or imagination,' they continue.

'I have always been free and have never felt suppressed. And how do you explain the knowledge of spiritual matters in someone like me who had not even received an hour of catechism? Does that come from my imagination? Also what about the conversions of so many people who have been exposed to these Messages? Is that caused by my imagination as well?'

Some clergy have decided that all these mysterious happenings were not my imagination or encounters with God, but rather tricks of the devil, as my old friend Fr. Jim had thought. But to those critics I say, 'Has Satan converted then? Because these encounters have converted me to loving and serving God, and have done the same to many others. I never had any intention of changing my life before this began. Would Satan want me and thousands of others to convert to God like this? Who else but God could have transformed me and so many others? Who other than God could have healed the sick and cast out demons? Who else could have been calling us, loving us, warning us?'

Thankfully, while some religious leaders have doubted the Messages, many others have embraced them. Still others are taking a 'wait and see' approach. There is no scientific method for distinguishing between what is natural and what is supernatural, what is considered 'of God' as opposed to 'not of God'. Church authorities normally do not take a stand on personal revelations like mine as long as the person who's receiving them is still alive. Just as we cannot evaluate a book on the basis of a few quotations given out of context, so the Church also waits until the totality of the person's work is complete.

I know it is hard for people to accept that a person like me would get Messages from God. I don't blame people for doubting. But when they see the 'fruit' of this work, I wish they would rejoice and give glory to God for the graces He is giving to people.

In addition to the Messages I receive, there are other supernatural occurrences I can share.

Some time ago we made a pilgrimage to the Holy Land. While sailing on the Sea of Galilee, several Swedes from our group asked me to give a short talk. We got together in one of the sitting rooms and during our discussion it seems that I said, in a very convincing way, 'I must go up north and witness to the people there.' I meant that I intended to travel further north than Sweden. They looked up surprised and one of them said, laughing:

'There is nobody up there, only bears and reindeer!'

I was told later that I stared back at him and said, very solemnly,

'Yes, there is one soul up there.'

Anyone who knows me well is fully aware that I hate cold weather. I am a 'Mediterranean and desert' person. For this reason it would have been out of character for me to travel to places that polar bears call home. Nevertheless, after the trip, when we were all back home, as I prepared supper one evening, one of the Swedes telephoned me to say,

'You were quite right on the boat. There is a person up there in Lapland who has called, inviting you to give your testimony.'

I was quite puzzled.

'What are you talking about?'

As far as I could recall I had never mentioned Lapland, or anything to do with its frozen landscape. Hearing my disbelief the caller insisted, relating everything that had been said during our little talk on the Sea of Galilee.

I gave a knowing sigh and put the receiver down. I knew very well who was behind this one! So be it; it was not a big deal for God to send me where the bears and reindeers lived.

Clearly God had arranged it this way to make it happen. Since He could not count on me to willingly get my boots and parka on and head toward the North Pole, He put the words into my mouth and my friends held me to them. God has a great, holy sense of humor and knows us well. At such times I know there is no point in arguing, so I shrugged my shoulders and waited for Lapland's invitation. It came soon after, and off I went to meet our Lap brothers and sisters.

On arrival, accompanied by a friend, we looked around to see who was meeting us, and spotted a joyful, plump lady who ran across the arrival hall to welcome us. We drove straight to our hotel to lunch there together with a Reverend from Stockholm and his friend. The restaurant was empty, which made me wonder where the townspeople were, and how many would be at the venue for the witnessing meeting. The Reverend and his friend were still drinking their coffee when I was called to leave for the meeting hall.

When they finally left the restaurant they were late, so they needed to walk briskly to reach the hall. As they hurried along the empty roads they saw an old man strolling towards them. It was as though he stumbled upon them. Recognizing that they were not from his town he called to them as he passed by:

'My good fellows, where are you from?'

'From Stockholm.'

'But why are you in such a rush, my good men?' the old man insisted.

'We are in a rush to go and listen to a prophet.'

'A prophet, in our town?' You could have knocked the old man out with a feather; he was so amazed.

'Yes, and we're late, do you want to come too?'

'All my life I've believed that prophets are only found in the Bible. Are you telling me that they are still around – and in my own town?'

'Do you want to come or not?' both cried out to him impatiently.

'Yes, I'm coming!'

Close to a hundred people gathered at the hall and listened attentively to my witnessing. Many of them were cut to the heart. Southerners often regard the Nordic people as being rather cold and expressionless, so it was amazing to see so many with tears streaming down their faces, showing how deeply the Messages had touched them.

It sometimes happens that God does not speak to us Himself, but uses emissaries. He may use the most unlikely people to communicate with us, or even take the place of a friend or a stranger. He may send an Angel, who takes on human form, to pass on His Message.

I remember how one day I met a complete stranger who knew nothing about me, but who passed on some words of hope when I most needed them. I had been told by the doctor treating me to stay in bed for three months because I had slipped discs in my back. I needed an MRI scan, so my friends drove me to the hospital and I was put in a wheelchair and waited with them in a large corridor. A ragged, unshaven man approached my friends, wanting to sell handkerchiefs and lighters. After one of my friends made a few purchases he moved off. Before he had gone far, however, he suddenly turned back and walked straight up to me. Looking me straight in the eyes, he said,

'The doctors here are very good and you will be all right soon, because *your mission* is not yet over.'

I was dumbfounded and so were my friends. Neither I, nor they, had ever seen this man before, and he certainly didn't know anything about me. I was growing slightly wiser in the ways of God and I understood that the stranger's words were offered from somewhere far beyond the hospital. Whether we realize it or not, and no matter the circumstances, supernatural or absolutely mundane, God never leaves us on our own – we are never abandoned.

This was not the only time our Lord encouraged me. One day I was invited to give my testimony in the English countryside. A local priest had given permission for me to speak in the parish hall and then hold Mass in the church next door. It was a mid-week meeting, held on a winter's evening when the sky was dark. I remember the meeting so well.

As I spoke I looked at the faces of those present and my eyes constantly fell on people yawning. There were over two hundred present, and all I could see were mouths wide open, yawning, which I found depressing. Of course they had worked all day, but it was a distraction and I felt that perhaps, the Holy Spirit had not inspired my witnessing. No one moved, they simply looked tired and worn out.

After my talk I was sad, somewhat put off, and felt that the message had not gotten through to the people. I was thinking from a human perspective, instead of God's perspective. With a tinge of self-pity I inwardly moaned to myself, 'All this sacrifice and all this traveling, staying up late at night, standing up there for almost two hours, I'm totally worn out!'

At the end of my talk everyone slowly moved over to a door that led to the church for Mass. It was almost ten o'clock, and I entered last. Everyone was seated and the benches were full. Continuing my complaining I thought, 'Why, thanks very much for your consideration, everyone! You didn't even leave a seat for me.'

I stood facing the crowd, looking for a place, when I saw a young boy about ten years old standing and signaling to me to go over to join him. He was in the second row on the left-hand side of the church, so I dragged myself over to him and discovered that he had kept a place for me. Seated at the other end of the bench I saw an Asian man – the boy was in between us.

I thought, 'This is late for him; where are his parents?' but the boy seemed to be alone. It was a school night, so I wondered how he could be out this late, when the boy slid along the bench to be close to me and picked up my hands. While holding them, he pointed to a Rosary ring on my finger and asked me, 'What is this?' I answered, 'It's a Rosary ring.' Then he pointed to another finger where I was wearing yet another Rosary ring. He asked again, saying, 'And this?' I replied, 'This is another Rosary ring, given to me by a visionary.'

I thought that by now he must think I'm a freak, filling my fingers with Rosaries. Every time I spoke he looked at me, and I noticed that he had big, almond shaped, greenish blue eyes. Then the priest came and started Holy Mass. By then, helped by the boy's presence, I felt somewhat happier.

As we sang the opening hymn, the priest's housekeeper, sitting right behind us, sang so loudly and out of tune that the boy giggled and so did I. In fact I had to hold myself back from laughing aloud. Finally, it was Holy Communion time, and as I stood, turning to the boy, ready to follow him to the Altar rail, he disappeared in front of my eyes – poooff! The boy simply vanished. I couldn't believe it! I did not see him again in the church.

When the Lord gives the gift of prophecy, He adds another gift, and that is the gift of discernment. These two gifts go hand in hand and I must say that the gift of discernment, of being able to 'discern' the spirits, or assess the origin and intention of spirits, has been very important. Here is one example.

On a visit to the Philippines, not my first, where I had been invited to speak, I heard about a young Filipino girl aged around fourteen. I was told that she, too, was receiving Messages from Christ. People were delighted that one of their own had received this gift and told me that her Messages were very similar to those I received. They brought her along wherever we went – she was around me the whole time.

When I had fulfilled my planned witnessing and other events, there was just one day left to be together with the organizers and other friends. The priest who had accompanied me took the opportunity to offer Mass for us all.

Standing next to the young girl during Mass, I thought that I should give her something of mine. I was wearing a Rosary ring, and to be frank, I did not really like it. It was metal and I intended to get one in either silver or gold. It was also very tight for my finger and as she was smaller, I thought that maybe I could give the ring to her. I tried to pull it off my finger, but it would not move. I decided that later on, during the lunch break I would go to the rest room, soap my finger and then be able to pull it off.

Mass was over and the girl accompanied us to the restaurant. We were all seated when I remembered the ring. I placed my hands on the table to get up and saw that the ring was gone! It had disappeared from my finger. It could not have slipped off because it was far too tight. I gasped, and the priest, noticing my bewilderment, asked me what was wrong. I told him what had happened. He calmly said, 'The Virgin Mary did not want to give that ring to the person you intended. She took it away.'

This immediately aroused my suspicion, and I asked to see the young girl's Messages to check their validity. Reading them, I saw that she was copying the Messages I was receiving. Even her 'Angel' had the same name as my Angel. So that was it. I told the story to my Filipino friends who were shocked. Later, after I had left the Philippines, I found out that this girl was an imposter, and eventually nobody followed her. She was revealed. I understood how the Lord had protected me from being deceived.

Sometimes I used to think, 'I wish He could lift the veil a little, the veil that Jesus once said He had put on me when He was with me. I would like to see what is behind the veil!' But God's Wisdom is infinite and He knows what He is doing. God knew all along that if He were to lift that veil completely I would surely die. My whole body, mind, and everything would collapse.

One day He lifted the veil just a little bit. It was one of the most awesome mystical experiences I have ever had and could never forget! What happened was undeservedly glorious.

10

Lifting the Veil

One night I happened to be alone. My son was asleep in bed and my husband was away, working in Africa. It was late. The traffic outside had diminished and I was sitting on the living room carpet. I was taking down a Message from Jesus and as He talked to me I suddenly asked, 'Can't You just lift the veil slightly so that I may see You?'

Without warning, Jesus did as I had asked! At that moment I felt, more powerfully than ever before, this awesome, magnificent Presence all around me. The overwhelming power of this Mighty God came upon me like a thunderbolt, crushing me flat to the floor! I lay there for some time, incapable of standing. I no longer felt the Presence of 'a Someone', but instead in a flash I saw something frightening in its power, terrible, overwhelming. I found myself shaking, but not from fear. I had been jolted by the sheer inexplicable power I had experienced. My whole being was permeated with God's Mightiness and Greatness. Everything around me ceased to have any relevance and the totality of my very being was suddenly focused on one massive, all-enveloping crescendo of transcendent bliss.

I had not realized that tears were running down my cheeks. I was not weeping; they were tears of awe. Weakened by this powerful vision I looked around, through my tears, and saw the quantity of notebooks containing God's Messages. Suddenly a new awareness swept over me as everything became crystal clear. I asked myself, 'Have I really written all these with God – how can this be?' It was then that I became totally aware and conscious that God was genuinely guiding me, and the notebooks truly did contain the words of the Almighty!

If before there had been the slightest remnant of doubt, in a flash it was gone.

Then, in that instant, I had an image of the whole universe. The vast expanse of everything seemed like nothing, really nothing in size or wonder compared to God's awesome power and greatness. I realized that God is undeniably the All Powerful Spirit of the spirit order and the Creator of it, which He created 'out of nothing' (*ex-nihilo*). He is Eternal. He is Master of All and for Him the Universe is like a speck of dust. And yet, this great God contains so much simplicity, meekness, love and mercy that none of us could ever come close to understanding it! It became clear to me that if God wanted to, He could easily crush the entire universe with just a thought and the whole of creation would collapse and disappear!

When we think of Jesus Christ, we can relate to Him because He has the form of a Man. We forget His power, His omnipotence, and that He is God as well.

With this supernatural awareness I understood that the whole earth is nothing in the sight of God! Yet, that Great God who encompasses all beings without being contained by their limits comes with His Heart in His Hand to offer it to me, *to us all!* He speaks openly with plain words, not in dark corners, and His Voice is music to my ears. He addresses us with religion and poetry and with majestic authority; His thoughts enlighten my intellect to understand the hidden sense of His proverbs. In His smiles and His delight He unseals mysterious sayings that were kept hidden from our eyes in the Book of Life.

I also came to understand after hearing Him talk, that God is also a poet, an artist! He Himself once confirmed it in one of His Messages:

> *'In these times of Grace I come with Mercy and I address you with poetry. My Words uttered are religion and virtue. With oil of gladness I anoint all those who approach Me, sealing them on their foreheads.'*[1]

The way He creates beauty and nature as well with all its different amazing colors signifies to me that God 'has good taste', and He

---

1 May 21, 2001

enjoys what He does; neither does He hide His satisfaction when He creates things, for all that He creates He calls 'good' and feels happy about it. Above all, God delights to give us all these 'good' things that He creates, freely, to enjoy them and share with us the magnificence of His creation.

As quickly as this experience started, it ended. Jesus told me:

> *'See how you felt and why I have your eyes veiled? You would not have been able to circulate normally. I only lifted the corner of the veil, not the entire veil.'*

I thanked our Lord for having given me all those graces and the gift without my meriting them. I started to understand that God will never leave me alone in this mission, remembering certain words He had spoken, such as:

> *'Announce My Holy Works, honor Me by exposing My Light on the roof of your house so that everyone may see It. Let It be seen by all; when they will perceive this Light, they will assemble from far and wide; let them know how I came to you giving you this Light.'*[2]

After this vision, life carried on as normal until one day a friend of mine asked me whether I was interested in attending some classes based on mystical theology given by a theologian. Apparently this theologian was an expert in this field. This attracted me because I assumed his explanations would give me a greater understanding of my own situation. My friend had previously informed the theologian of my experiences and he was interested to the point of offering to translate the Messages from English to French. The theologian saw fit to introduce me to the monks in a Benedictine monastery situated high in the Swiss Alps. He was well known to them and they had provided him with a cell for his time of meditation when visiting them.

I looked forward to meeting the holy monks. After having been introduced to them, they were keen to hear my story. After

---

2 January 24, 1988

listening to me they rejoiced that God had blessed me, giving Messages for our times. They invited me to visit them often so that we could pray together. Some days later when I went back to them I offered the Superior a crucifix that was blessed in a special way by Jesus. This present delighted him, especially that it was blessed in such a special way.

However, things soon changed. The positive atmosphere did not last very long, because once again the devil interfered. I had learned that in order to discourage a soul, the devil will use both man and objects to achieve his goal. He turns everything to his advantage, using lies and deception to blind good people, turning them into persecutors of the soul he is after. The devil not only uses human weakness to create tribulations, confusion, and disputes but also uses the laws of nature to his advantage to create noise and all the way to catastrophes. This is what happened in that monastery.

The monks knew an elderly lady whom they considered 'their mystic'. She too claimed to have real experiences of God, and had been leading the monastery and guiding the monks for years. The monks, delighted, introduced me to her, and what should have been a friendly meeting to share our experiences turned out rather differently. She seemed displeased that I was there at all. The whole encounter was more of an interrogation than a friendly meeting. Her coldness and hostility towards me did not fit the image I had made of her as a mystic and her rigid attitude caught me unaware and I was very hurt.

Obviously, she did not appreciate the interest the monks showed in me. To get me away from the monastery, which she clearly considered as her territory, she told the monks that I was an evil bluffer. She said that all my claims about the Messages and my relationship with God and Jesus were a hoax. She told the Superior to get rid of the crucifix I had given him as quickly as possible, because it had evil powers. I heard later on that he believed her and threw it from a monastery window, down the cliff.

This grieved me a great deal. I believe this woman thought my presence would result in her losing control and authority over the monks, but of course that was never my intention. This incident upset my friend the theologian to such an extent that he no longer visited the mountaintop monastery. And from then on the Superior of that monastery did everything he could to turn people against me, both in Switzerland and abroad.

He even contacted a renowned Italian priest, giving him misinformation, thereby discrediting the Messages. By grace, this Italian priest received Messages from the Virgin Mary, destined for priests in the present times, and had created a movement for the priesthood based on his charism. For this reason he was well known around the world and trusted by many priests and bishops who followed his movement. It so happened that the Superior was responsible for the movement in Switzerland, and his misinformation resulted in the Italian priest doing a great deal of harm on an international scale, turning many of his priests against God's Messages.

Fr. Bordeau, a holy monk from the United States, had been given photocopies of some of the Messages and read them with great interest. Unfortunately, he spoke to the Italian priest, who told him the Messages were from the devil, calling out '*diabolo!*' in Italian. Later, I learned that when Fr. Bordeau had heard this, he was saddened beyond description, because the Messages had spoken to his heart. He had truly sensed God in them.

A few days after receiving that blow, Fr. Bordeau was invited to go to Medjugorje, a small village in Croatia where the Virgin Mary was appearing daily to five young children, and where millions have gone to pray. With a heavy heart, he traveled to the site, and asked God for a sign. He prayed, 'Lord, if Vassula is from You and You are truly giving her Messages, I would like to receive a bouquet of flowers today, as a sign.'

Having said this prayer he went to join other priests who were hearing confessions outside Medjugorje's famous church. Suddenly, a very tall man holding a bouquet of wild flowers approached him. He stared at the flowers in amazement, and full of awe he asked, 'What are these flowers?'

The stranger replied, 'They are for you – take them.' Still amazed at such a quick response from God, he managed to ask, 'Where did you get them?'

The man replied, 'While I was going on a stroll this morning, I noticed some children playing in the field. When they noticed me they began to collect wild flowers, and then ran up to me to offer them to me.'

Bearing no doubts any more in his heart and recognizing how God had answered his prayer, this monk became a great apostle for the Messages in the United States.

When Easter came, Jesus led me to understand that the Benedictine monk's uncharitable and negative attitude towards me and His Messages was grieving Him a lot.

Jesus asked me to write to the monk, asking him to make peace. In spite of all the wounds the monk had inflicted on me by spreading slander and calumny, I was willing to forgive him and let him know that I held no grudge against him.

Encouraged by Jesus I wrote him an Easter postcard. He did not reply. I believe the Lord was giving him a chance because of what was about to happen.

Meanwhile the Italian priest, whom the Swiss monk had misinformed, discovered the truth about me from a reliable source, a renowned theologian, Msgr René Laurentin whose opinion on the Messages was and still is very favorable. The Italian priest was upset about having been misinformed. The next time he traveled through Switzerland he called his interpreter, who happened to be the very same Swiss monk, and rebuked him for having misled him. This was embarrassing for the poor monk, but that was not the end of the situation.

The next day the Italian priest was holding a public meeting for lay people. My friends were going and asked me to join them. I was not sure whether I should go, but their insistence convinced me to attend.

Right in the middle of the Italian priest's speech, he said that no one should persecute me and that each person has been granted his own gift from God, which is known as a charism. He went on to say that anyone is free to follow any individual who has obtained a charism from God such as prophecy or the gift of healing or the gift of knowledge or other gifts. He warned, however, never to mix them – meaning that each charism should operate on its own. I noticed how the monk blushed as he was forced to interpret those words about me. After the talk I went to the Italian priest to thank him. He was standing close to the monk, and although short in stature he managed to grab the monk by his neck, lowering him to his size and said, 'Now, in front of me, hug her and kiss her and make peace with her!' As we hugged the monk whispered in my ear, 'I received your card but I don't intend to answer it.'

In the meantime the theologian became so disgusted with the monk's inflexibility and his continual persecution of me that he gave up his cell at the monastery.

Some years later this monk fell gravely ill. A friend of mine, who knew him, often went to the monastery to keep him company during his illness. During every visit she told him about my mission, and how it was progressing, and spoke of the good fruits it was bearing. In the end before dying, he accepted his mistake and repented. I saw God's hand in that, because the dying monk asked my friend to bring him the Message books again. This was a lesson to me because I learned how God, in His great Mercy, always gives us a chance to repent and be forgiven before we die.

One bright day, with the smell of spring in the air and a perfect blue sky, I decided to eat my lunch outside on our small veranda facing Lake Leman. As I began to eat, I saw with the eyes of my soul Jesus, sitting on the chair near me, staring at my food. I felt rather uncomfortable since at first He did not utter a word. I stopped eating. Pointing at my plate with His chin He asked me,

'Is this good?'

'Oh yes, Lord!' I blurted out, feeling embarrassed with some food still in my mouth.

'Don't you want me to bless it?'

He asked. I understood and managed to say,

'Yes Lord …'

He blessed the food and remained with me till I finished eating, and by so doing He made me understand that I should thank Him at the end of my meal, which I did. I am convinced the Lord appeared in this way to show me how eager He is to give all of us His blessings.

I had been sending copies of the Messages to my sister in Rhodes for some time and she had become a true apostle of the Messages there. She regularly shared the Messages with her friends and neighbors who were keen to listen to her and to read the Messages. Many who had been negligent in their spiritual life became fervent Christians and returned to the Church. My sister was on fire and nothing would stop her from spreading the Messages. She even phoned old friends of hers in Switzerland and told them about my experiences.

That led to one of them calling me and asking to meet me, so I invited her over to my flat. I told her my story and while I was speaking I noticed that now and then she was looking in one direction – towards a cabinet where I kept all my notebooks. In the end, she asked me where the roses were that were perfuming the sitting room so strongly, as she couldn't see any around. I told her there were no roses. She said that her nose was 'burning' from the scent of roses. As I opened the cabinet to show her my notebooks, she stood up, saying,

'That's where the fragrance of roses comes from!'

During all that time I smelled nothing. She was so taken by her experience that the first thing she did when back at the office was to tell her colleagues all about it. Her boss was very interested and asked if he could come over with her to meet me. He was more interested in hearing about Jesus than experiencing a supernatural sign.

Her boss was an Italian by birth and had lived in Switzerland for most of his life. He was a typical playboy, spending his time in casinos, partying, and dining in sophisticated company. Although a Roman Catholic he seldom went to his church since his faith had withered. The minute they entered my home they both smelled incense and asked me whether I had perfumed the flat. I assured them I had no incense. He took this as a sign from God. It was late at night when they both left and instead of going straight home, still intrigued with his experience, he entered the first church he found open. When he entered, the lights were off and seeing nobody there, he felt creepy. He walked along the empty aisle towards the Altar and knelt in front of

Christ. Filled with emotion he asked Him seven personal questions and requested a sign. At that very moment he heard a creaking sound at the back. But he said to God, 'That is not good enough to make me believe.'

So, he got up and left. In the meantime I had no idea that he had been to a church, neither did I know that he had asked Jesus questions. Early the next morning Jesus called me and asked me to write down a Message for him. I called his office and told him that he had a Message from Christ and should come over to take it. I had forgotten that people feel shocked when they hear they have received a Word directly from God and I, in my forgetfulness, had informed him in a very casual way.

I still smile when I remember the look on his face when I opened the door to him. He had that sort of beaten up look – his eyes full of guilt. Given the way he had left the church the night before, he was probably expecting the strongest words of reproach from Christ. He was hunched over, and seemed to have shrunk in size so much that he no longer looked as tall as he actually was. It was as though he wanted the earth to open and engulf him! I really don't know how he managed to shrink that much. He came in without a word, and when I gave him the Message I noticed his hand tremble.

I noticed how his whole complexion started to brighten up and gradually change, as though a light was cast on him while he was reading the Message. He was still in shock and said lamely, 'Christ has answered all seven of my questions of last night.'

From that moment, his life completely changed. He felt forgiven. He became a staunch Christian and a witness to the love of Christ. In his newfound joy, he wanted his best friend who lived nearby in France to find God as well. He called his friend, who was no less a playboy than he himself had been, and asked him to come over to Switzerland for the weekend. But when his friend heard he had discovered God, he was not at all happy. The one who accompanied him to the casinos and wild parties every night was now talking about God? The horror!

But in the end, the Frenchman accepted the weekend invitation and with great reluctance agreed to come to my place to meet me, whom he was already calling 'the Hag' as if I were some kind of witch.

When they arrived at my house, the Frenchman saw me looking like a normal, sporty woman, in jeans and a white T-shirt, at which point he dropped the 'hag' bit. During our initial encounter, however, he remained silent as a tomb. I offered them dinner on the veranda. After dinner I went over to the cabinet and took out one of the notebooks to show him the handwriting of the Messages. He had still not uttered a word. He took it in his hands and rapidly turned the pages before handing it back to me, whereupon I went inside and placed it on the low table in the sitting room.

Dinner over, I went out to collect the plates and as I passed where he had been sitting I smelled the most exquisite fragrance, right in that location. It seemed to be an invisible column of fragrance and outside that specific place there was no trace. I called them over to the perfumed spot. They came out into the veranda and after smelling, our friend from France said placidly, 'Yes, this is the perfume that came from your notebook.'

I knew that he thought I had perfumed my notebook, so I said, 'I never perfume my notebooks; this is a sign for you to believe.' I took him by the hand and led him to my notebook, still lying on the sitting room table, and asked him to pick it up and smell it. I knew that he would smell nothing, and indeed, he smelled nothing.

He was the type of guy who does not show his feelings, but inside, he was torn. When they left, he asked to stop by any church, and to his friend's amazement, without any embarrassment he knelt down and prayed. Christ had instantly restored his faith just by a small sign, revealing Himself by a mere fragrance.

God knew what the man needed, and that sign was just the thing. God adapts Himself marvelously to each person. He knows what we need, and when. He approaches us in a way that will best get our attention – sometimes through tenderness, so as not to scare us, and other times in more dramatic ways that will 'wake us up'. The plenitude of God is poured out upon each creature. In our times that are so difficult, where rationalism and materialism have taken over every aspect of spiritual life, making unbelievers of the once faithful and invading their minds with everything except God, yet the God they have forgotten has never forgotten them. God Himself says:

'Tell them that the God they have forgotten has never forgotten them.'[3]

God is extending His Divine Mercy, adapting Himself to descend on our so impoverished spiritual life with unmerited gifts to us. God is in search of each and every soul, as He says:

'I happened to be taking a walk nearby a river when I saw a driftwood, drifting away with the worldly current; I leaned over and picked it out of the stream, I brought it Home with Me and planted it in My Garden of Delights; from a dry piece of wood I made out of you a Tree. I said: "Grow! Grow and take root in My Garden, in My own Property, and from your blossoms exhale a perfume to appease My Justice." I said: "Crops of fruit shall sprout each month and your leaves will be the cure to many." Now and then I amuse Myself in pruning you. My delight is to see flowers in blossom and a constant growth in your fruit; alone, the Water from My Sanctuary can give you growth and Life. I, Yahweh, will see to it that you prosper; I take pleasure in picking now and then on My way pieces of driftwood; I can give life to anything I pick on My way.'[4]

3 May 27, 1993; January 28, 1995; August 19, 1996

4 November 13, 1991

11

Visions and Signs

Visions such as the Dove became constant. All the visions that were given to me proceeded from the fountain of Divine Wisdom and were a gift from the Holy Spirit. Most of the visions were symbolic and many came to reality.

Over the years, I've had many meetings with friends who were interested in learning more about God's actions. They always had lots of questions, and I did my best to answer them. Here are some of those conversations.

'I would like to know, before we speak about visions and signs, more of God's personality; can you tell us something from your experiences?'

First off, God adapts language and approach to the one to whom He is speaking. It's not that He changes – as God is unchanging. It's that ALL personality is from God. He is infinitely creative, so He can draw from His infinite treasure chest of characteristics to relate to the person with whom He's communicating. This is for the sake of the instrument so they can understand what He's saying; in that way we're speaking the 'same language'.

When I hear God speak, wow! His words are just like poetry! There's no doubt that God is The Poet, and The Artist, and in reading His Messages we find this poetic language in every page. Some of His words remind us of Hymns. He even calls His Messages now and then, '*My Love Hymn*'.

The Bible is the Love Letter of God. The way He creates beauty and nature as well with all its different shapes and colors, the colors of the rainbow, for example, signifies to me that God loves beauty and His Majesty enjoys what He creates. When you look at certain creatures – like funny birds – one must have a sense of humor. Why does He create these funny creatures? Because at the same time as being Pure Light and Sovereign of All, He's a joyful God, a smiling God, He's happy. God does not hide His satisfaction when He creates things, for all that He creates He says to Himself: 'This is good.' And, don't forget, those good things He creates are for *us!* He delights to give all these good things freely so that we enjoy them and share with Him the magnificence of His creation.

Twice I have seen Jesus wink at me from a fresco of the Almighty that is painted on the dome of the Greek Orthodox churches. Both times were when I felt that there was 'no solution' to a situation I was going through. When I lifted my eyes and looked at the fresco of the Almighty, He suddenly winked at me. A friend standing near me, the first time this happened, had also seen His eye wink. Both times, the difficult situation, immediately after that humorous sign, were solved immediately. I understood with that wink that Christ was telling me, 'Just wait and see what I'll do …'

In the beginning when I had learned to say properly the 'Our Father', while God Himself was listening, just after a few days, He asked me. '*Do you have anything to give Me?*' So I started to think what I could give God that would please Him. God interrupted me and said, '*Anything good you will give Me, comes from Me.*' I wanted to think of something I had of my own to give Him. I said, 'I know, I can paint You a painting – an icon and give it to the Church.' '*The gift of art Vassula, it also comes from Me.*' Of course, I thought, so I said, 'Then I have nothing of my own to give You.' '*You have,*' God answered. '*Give Me your will.*' 'My will? But I have given it to You a week ago!' '*Yes, little one, but I like to hear it every day!*'

Above all, my answer is that God is Majesty, Sovereignty, a Figure of Wonder, and wholly Beautiful. Even the very moon lacks brightness in His Glory. God is resplendent and without parallel. When He speaks, He speaks with Majesty.

The soul would like to ask Him, as I did: 'where are You leading me?' He answered: '*To the Truth*'. On another occasion I asked, 'Where have You mingled me?' '*Into My Body*', was His reply. He brought me to penetrate into His Mystical Body, which is the Church.

'Now tell us what kinds of visions you have had.'

I have experienced numerous visions of several kinds. Those of spiritual substance made my soul perceive elements that do not have corporeal bodies, such as Angels, lights, truths, souls, and God Himself. Other visions that I have experienced have concerned hidden or future events and some of these have already taken place. To forewarn us, God has given prophecies. Visions of my own soul have been given to me so that I can see the state of my soul. Visions of Heaven, Purgatory and Hell have also been shown to me.

Visions given in my intellect or in dreams come to me unexpectedly and spontaneously, when God wishes. The eyes of my soul perceive only the things that God wishes me to see and understand. One of the most magnificent visions that were ever given to me which left me in awe was this of God the Father. God the Father allowed me to see Him as He is. I was short of words to describe the magnificence of the Father. I know that many people would have liked to see God, but if we do see God, Scriptures say we shall die. However this was only a vision and it is different. This is what I wrote in my notebooks on September 25, 1997 while I was invoking Yahweh's Name:

'Suddenly a Figure of wonder, looking just like the Son of Man in His glorious transfiguration, Yahweh the Lord of lords appeared to me vested in full splendor; His heavenly robe shimmering and yet colorless; glittering as though covered by diamonds and other precious stones. And while I was staring, bewildered and mystified, on this enchanting vision of grace and incomparable beauty, when Yahweh, delicately emerged from behind the clouds, doing it with such a graceful movement, I felt my heart blossoming.

'His Majesty reminded me of a bridegroom stepping out of a pavilion; His Presence radiated a gracefulness that even if I tried to describe it all my life I would never manage; His Presence at the same time radiated love and so much sweetness and tenderness that my soul was swept to the ground; His beautiful Head was leaning slightly to the right, like those Sacred Heart statues; "You are beautiful, my God, although I can only peer through a veil, I see Your hair in dark locks reaching Your shoulders, and Your beautiful Face, the pallor of ivory, is enchanting to the eye;" I blurted out. Yahweh's posture was though of someone timid, but do not mistake me, it was not ...

'What must it be like to contemplate You all day long in Heaven with our bare eyes? How and where shall I find sufficient words to describe Your Grace and Your Beauty? Words surpass me, especially that slight movement You made, to step out from behind the clouds ...'

On another occasion, while I was receiving a Message from Christ, unexpectedly, an amazing manifestation of the Holy Trinity was given to me. Looking at Jesus, I saw distinctly two other Persons come out of Him simultaneously: one from His left side and the other from His right side. I knew I was looking at the Holy Trinity that has mutual love, communication and knowledge. In an instant I understood that all three Persons, who are one God alone, have but one Will, one Power, one Dominion. They disappeared as suddenly as They had appeared, entering in the figure of Christ once more. In the end, although Three, we have only One Creator: 'Three in One and One in Three.'

'Have you had any visions of Heaven or Purgatory?'

On March 26, 1987 God called me, saying in a few words that Heaven was created by measuring every width, height and depth and all dimensions were perfect. He went on to say that every little living creature came from Him and all is His. He said that all Life comes from Him, and His Breath is Life. Then gently, He asked me whether I wished to learn more about His heavenly works, to which I answered 'Yes, Lord'. Then He said,

'Let us have a walk in My Glory.'

I found myself in spirit walking with God's Presence in a beautiful, very colorful Garden. The light was plentiful and bright, but did not come from a normal sun. While walking I noticed an enormous ball of light almost touching the horizon. It was like a big sun, but one could look at it without burning the eyes. God asked me,

'How do you feel, daughter?'

Feeling absolutely amazed, I said: 'It is beautiful; it's all strange!'

He asked,

> *'What can you see?'*

'This sort of sun.'

> *'Yes, it is My Holy Abode; and what can you see around the Light?'*

At first it appeared to me that there were spots moving around the 'sun'. There was a movement for sure, but then looking more closely these 'spots' turned out to be myriads of Angels encircling the Light. God said,

> *'They are Cherubim encircling My Glory. What else do you see?'*

Feeling hesitant, I said, 'Some steps leading into the "sun"?

> *'Let us enter this Light. Are you ready? Take off your shoes for we are entering on holy ground. We are now inside the Light.'*

I thought that once inside the Light I would find myself in extreme brightness, but to my surprise, everything inside was of a blue color. What struck me most, however, was the silence and the feeling of peace and holiness in the air. It was amazing! A huge circle surrounded me. The 'wall' was not a wall, but living creatures. They were Angels; a wall of Angels standing close to each other, as though stuck to one another and one on top of the other all the way up, closing the 'dome'; beautiful, tall Angels and they were all of a blue color. There were millions, myriads, of them standing erect and in silence with their hands together as though in worship. The Lord said,

> *'My Seraphim are guarding this Holy Place and are worshipping Me incessantly. Can you hear them?'*

Suddenly I heard: 'Holy of Holies, Holy is our God Most High'. God, drawing my attention elsewhere, said,

> *'And who is this with the gold sword and so beautiful?'*

I saw another Angel who differed from the others, because He was of 'normal color'. He was standing right in the middle of the 'circle' and was dressed in a long, shimmering robe of the purest white. He had golden, shoulder length hair and was holding a beautiful Golden Sword. God said,

'The sword is My Word; My Word is pure; It pierces and illuminates.'

Suddenly I saw the 'dome' opening in the way a flower opens. God exclaimed,

'Behold, little one, try to discern ... You will see above you now the Holy Battle that is to come. O daughter, keep a vigilant look around you and be aware that evil exists. Can you see anything?'

When this 'dome' opened I saw a huge image. It was as though a zoom was used to draw everything closer to me. There were horses above with velvety black, fearful eyes. I saw only the eyes and part of their faces. The image went further away as though the zoom went backwards. I saw a battle in action between the Good Angels and the bad angels. The Lord said,

'My army will combat Satan and his followers, including all those that tried to destroy My Law. Remember that I am the Alpha and the Omega, the First and the Last. My Word is everlasting. Now what can you see?'

'I see a reptile like a big snake that was thrown from a horse.'

God said,

'This dragon under the lance of My Saint[1] *will be conquered. When this will be done, all his followers will fall too. Vassula, you will come now to see My Hall of Judgment.'*

I saw a big hall, but no one was there yet. Suddenly, I heard the clatter of chains coming from one corner. I looked around and saw a small group of souls, 'dead people'. They seemed haggard beyond

1 God refers to St Michael

description, stained with black as though they had been rolling in charcoal. They appeared to be unhappy and at the same time bewildered, uncertain as to their whereabouts. They did not seem to see us. God explained,

> *'Have you seen this multitude of souls? They have just arrived from underground. These are tormented souls who have been released. They were at Satan's gates.'*[2]

'Who released them?'

> *'I did, with My Heavenly Works and all who amend and love Me. You see why I want you to love Me? The deeper you love Me the better chance they have to be lifted and come to Me ... What you saw was only an image of them. They were not really in My Hall [of the Last Judgment]. Souls are not judged until the end.'*

The explanation of the Message above is that there are two judgments. The first, or particular judgment, is that experienced by each individual at the time of his or her death, at which time God will decide where the soul will go; either to Heaven, Purgatory or Hell. The Last Judgment will occur after the Second Coming of Christ and after the resurrection of the dead and the reuniting of a person's soul with their own physical body.

God continued, telling me that when in Purgatory, these souls were helpless without our prayers and our good acts, for God uses everything good to liberate them from Purgatory and bring them to Heaven.

The sword in the hands of the Angel was representing God's Word; that His Word is Eternal, it is pure and it cuts and pierces. I learned that Heaven is a reality; that Angels and demons exist, and that in the future a spiritual battle will take place. It is happening even now, but in the end the devil and his adepts will lose that battle.

'Give us an example of the "mysteries" that God reveals to you.'

Once, while in meditation, I perceived briefly, not once, but several times, an overwhelming vision. I saw that *the whole universe* is *within*

---

2 The lowest purgatory

God and that He contains everything within Himself – all is in Him and nothing can fall outside Him. Whenever I did not share with others a vision given to me, the vision would return to me again and again, until I spoke and wrote about it, as the one of God containing everything within Himself.

'Have you also experienced the miraculous smell of roses or incense?'

Yes, these signs have often happened to me, or to those around me, or those in other places who are speaking about the Messages. What happens is that we smell roses or incense, even though there are none in the vicinity. This is a sign from God. Once, while I was on the road driving with some friends, I was speaking about God the Father when suddenly we were all perfumed with incense – it was all around us. This type of thing has happened many times. The fragrance of incense has manifested, either coming from the notebooks containing the Messages or simply permeating the air around us as we prayed or were sharing the Messages. Many people around have smelled these fragrances; they are a sign of God's Presence.

'Why would God give such signs?'

From the moment I entered into this mysterious 'world' and was given a task beyond my strength, God, being very aware of my weakness and my dependence on Him, has blessed me with a variety of supernatural manifestations of His Presence. My constant need for God is like a child's need to be always near its parent, and these signs are the Father's way of always reminding me He's there. And He always offers encouraging words:

> *'My child, although you are incapable to understand fully My Wisdom, I have been, and I am, your only Teacher; I am progressing you step by step, I am educating you in the Ways of Wisdom; I am guiding you in the paths of virtue; do not seek to turn to your left nor to your right, cling to all that I have given you.'*[3]

3 March 3, 1989

'Are these signs really necessary? Isn't it better to just believe without them?'

Whatever God does, I will always be thankful, and I will never question God in His Wisdom or put Him to the test! These signs are 'food' for the poor and the wretched; they are to revive our faith. God knows much better than we do when we need signs and why we need them. God's signs are not given to satisfy our curiosity, but are given to draw us into conversion. They are meant to lead us into an awareness of God and into repentance. They are given to bring us into a life of prayer. My experience taught me that God deals ever so patiently and gently with us, with all our whims, corruption and sin. I ask people, 'Have you seen the cemetery? All these lying underground also thought that they were indispensable.' The funny part is that in our ego and delusion many of us act as though we are so knowledgeable that no one could equal or contradict us: we have answers to everything. But in reality we know so little – or nothing at all. Much of what we do and say is little more than pretence. The truth is that all our notions, all our strivings are worthless unless we recognize where our abilities spring from and hold fast to the knowledge that everything real and truly inspirational comes from One Source, and that is from God. So when God gives us signs, we should respect them and not question them. God told me:

> *'My Signs are not given to you to make a sensation on this earth; I solemnly ask all those who are after the sensational to come to Me humbly and pray.'*[4]

Some years ago there was a man who had abandoned church and was reluctant to drive his wife to one of my meetings because he did not believe in the Messages I was receiving. When he finally drove his wife he looked from the window of his car and saw me, but he did not actually see me, but rather the Face of Jesus superimposed on my face! This completely surprised him, and it had the powerful effect of reviving his faith.

This supernatural sign has been experienced by many. I don't feel anything when it happens. Jesus though gave His reasons. Since there

4 March 3, 1989

were some people doubting that the Messages were truly from Christ, this is what He said:

> *'I God will be among you and you will see this sign on her.'*[5]
>
> *'I am the Author of "True Life in God" and I shall prove it by appearing in your place; it is My Father's gift to you and to others.'*[6]

'Don't you think it's strange that God would use you in that way?'

I am fully aware that I have been a horrible sinner, and I do not deserve to have the image of Jesus appear on me, as if I was like Him. Nevertheless, our Lord, who is Divine Truth and All Pure has chosen not only to prove that He is the Author of these Messages but when He appears to individuals it is because of the greatness of the love He has for us. Souls that have observed this glorious manifestation have burst into tears and repentance, and have been greatly strengthened in their faith.

The first time this sign ever happened I was in the Philippines. I had been invited there to give my testimony and pass on the Message of God. While I was speaking, I suddenly noticed that the organizers and their friends, all seated in the front two rows, were squinting, their eyes partly closed. As it was late in the evening, I thought they were falling asleep. Then I saw them looking at each other and whispering. After the meeting they came over to me and said, excitedly, 'We saw the Lord on you! Your face disappeared and we saw *Him* instead!'

I was shocked, but the Lord had told me that this would happen. He had said,

> *'My daughter, By the power of the Holy Spirit I have raised you, My child, to be in perfect union with Me and witness to the crowds in My Name, giving yourself to them to the utmost of your capacity; your fidelity pleases Me; this is why I will continue to build My Plan in you until it is completed … and*

5 My Angel Daniel, January 10, 1987

6 October 20, 1994

> *the poor will hear something never told before and will see My Holy Countenance on you and those who never knew Me will approach Me and those whose eyes were veiled will see all My glory … whosoever will be moved by My Spirit, who today blows everywhere, will be heir to My Kingdom and the Father will welcome him together with throngs of angels in Heaven. I bless you now; ic.'*[7]

There have been countless occasions when all sorts of people in different countries, without ever having heard of this phenomenon, have seen Christ's Holy Face on me, covering mine, and sometimes He appeared in His entirety. This phenomenon has not only been seen with the naked eye, but on several occasions it has appeared on video as well. Christ would appear and momentarily take my place just for those watching me – for them alone. If a person happened to be someone who has offended Christ, then He would appear wearing the crown of thorns with blood pouring from His forehead.

On one occasion in New York, I was invited to speak in a basketball stadium with large video screen projectors. There were four ladies present who did not believe in my gift. Convinced that I was an impostor and out to deceive people, they had decided to leave as a group, a few minutes into my talk. But as soon as I started to speak, they saw the Holy Face of Christ on one of the video screens, and my face on the other screen. Because I was speaking my lips were moving, but so were Christ's. Then suddenly, both screens showed Christ's Holy Face – but only half, for the other half was my face. Of course, one can imagine how they felt after that. They sat glued to the bench until the end. Full of remorse for having persecuted me, they came to tell me their story and asked me to forgive them. I laughed, told them it was okay and praised the Lord.

A woman once told me that while clicking from channel to channel on her TV remote control she came upon me speaking. She stayed on the channel and suddenly saw this miracle. She went running to a friend, telling her what she had seen and said, 'She must be speaking

---

7 December 27, 1994. The letters 'ic' are initials found usually on icons, and mean in Greek, Jesus Christ

the truth! I have to find that woman!' She and her friend did find me, and in finding me they found the Messages. Today, they are among the many who having read the Messages have totally changed their lives. They discovered 'the pearl', that is God.

The thirst for God will grow as never before in anyone who sees this Sign. When Love awakens, invading their heart, from then on God will make them participants in His Being. He will restore their sight and they will glorify Him for the rest of their lives, and He, in His graciousness, will compensate them. This was a promise given in a Message where He said,

> *'I tell you: no one who glorifies Me is let down by Me; no one who waters a parched land is ignored by Me; My Heart is too sensitive and pure not to be touched; My graciousness observes you like a mother, like a father, every aspect of your behaviour is observed by Me. I love you; have no doubt of My love …'*[8]

'What other signs have happened in your mission?'

Many others. I remember once I was in Brazil witnessing to an audience of about six thousand people, reading out to them a Message regarding the outpouring of the Holy Spirit:

> *'And My healing Water from My Breast, this stream that flows out of My Sanctuary, will fill you and make you wholesome. No man shall be able to arrest this Rivulet. The stream will keep on flowing profusely out of My Heart. It shall flow everywhere, breaking into several parts, separating into other and several Rivulets going into all directions and wherever this healing Water flows, everyone, sick, lame, blind, will be healed. Even the dead [spiritual] will come back to life again. No one will be able to stop Me from purifying you.'*[9]

To my surprise, out of nowhere, thick drops of water started to fall from above. They fell on me, on the paper in my hand and on

---

8 December 16, 1994

9 June 2, 1991

the entire tabletop in front of me. I stopped speaking and looked up, thinking that maybe the roof leaked and rain was coming in. It was not raining outside, only on me and on the table. People had noticed this event and were smiling and, feeling excited, were whispering to each other. However, as some priests were sitting right behind me, I thought that maybe one of them had sprinkled holy water. As soon as I had finished speaking I sat near a priest and as I sat there, heavy drops of water again dropped on me from above. I looked at the priest nearby who sat, looking blankly in front of him, not blinking an eye. I asked him, 'Have you seen this?' 'Yes,' he said, and remained silent. A moment later I asked, 'Did you sprinkle holy water on me?' 'No I didn't.' Silence reigned; end of conversation. 'But what are those drops of water then?' I insisted. 'Oh, those … It is a sign of the Presence of the Holy Spirit.'

For him it was totally normal. He spoke in a way like someone would say, 'the phone booth is around the corner.' Then he added as though it was no big deal, 'I have seen it very often in my church when I perform a baptism.' He reflected a while and then capped off the conversation by saying, 'You know, when you were walking in the hall and you lifted your eyes and looked at me, your face disappeared and I saw superimposed the Holy Face of Christ!'

On another occasion while visiting Dublin, Ireland, a small group and I were driving from place to place by minibus. I put on my headset to listen to music, not paying attention to anything else, simply looking straight ahead. A friend sitting next to me was praying the Jesus Prayer ('Lord Jesus Christ, Son of God, have mercy on me, the sinner'), and when she pronounced the words 'Jesus Christ …' she heard me say, 'I AM'. She was amazed by the majestic manner in which the words were pronounced and thought, 'Wow, she can really imitate Him …' Later, when I removed the earphones, my friend said: 'That was a great, "I Am" from you when I said, Jesus Christ!' Not understanding her I said in astonishment, 'I never said that; why should I?' But she insisted that these words came majestically from my mouth. In the end we both understood that it was not I, but the Lord who had spoken.

In His graciousness He showed us how He responds when we say the Jesus Prayer. It so happened that the previous day my friend was in doubt that Jesus ever heard her in her prayers. I understood that our Lord had spoken, using my mouth to confirm to her that He is always present, and hears our prayers. This is also to remind us that we must never use the Lord's Name in vain.

On a trip to Scotland, my friend Carol introduced me to a Benedictine monk. Having just met with a Cardinal in Rome to share Jesus' wish for the Christian Churches to unite, I said to him, 'Jesus' aim is to unite the Church and have us reconcile with one another. The true Unity of the Church would be that all his priests from all Church denominations gather around one Altar and celebrate the Holy Eucharist together.'

The monk strongly reacted and said that this would not be right. According to Carol, my face changed suddenly and bore a very grave expression. Taken by the Spirit of God, I turned around and stood in a rather awkward position, as the movement was made so sudden and out of my control. Pointing my index finger at him, almost touching his nose, and with authority that was not mine at all, I said, 'This is the way that men think, not the way God thinks.'

Both Carol, who knew me well, and the monk were taken aback, and even I was surprised at how my body had twisted around so quickly. I knew these words did not come from me. The monk also knew instantly, in his heart, that these words, spoken with such authority and power, did not come from me, but from the Almighty God.

Although these words were a challenge to his conservative ideas, the monk loved them because he knew that they came from Jesus. For days he kept asking Carol to repeat the words so as to remind him of this incident where God had spoken.

During that visit to Scotland I had to witness and address God's Message to the people of Edinburgh. Although there were great obstacles, I still managed to give my talk. The majority of the people in the hall were Roman Catholic, but there were also Protestants, sitting way back from the podium. Someone in the crowd, while waiting for me to address them, said: 'Who is this lassie? Why can't Vassula come out and speak!' The people around him said, 'But it *is* Vassula!' He was surprised, because my countenance suddenly looked very young.

As soon as I told the crowd that I would start with the Holy Rosary, the Protestants nodded to one another to leave the hall. They stood up and gave me a last look, but as they did so they were as though electrified, because what they saw was no longer me, but instead it was Christ Himself standing in my place. They stared, rubbing their eyes, and sat down again, shocked. They understood that Christ wanted them to remain and learn to pray the Rosary and listen to what the Lord had to say. They realized that I was carrying not only the Word of God, but also the Hail Mary and that this prayer should be respected.

In the early 1990s a nun invited me to give my testimony in the USA. She worked very hard to organize the meeting and underwent strong opposition and persecution from her own brother who was a priest. She did not give up, because she was convinced of the authenticity of the Messages of Christ. When I arrived, however, I found her downcast and low in spirits.

She welcomed me, hurrying to pick up my luggage before showing me to my room in the convent. As she put down the luggage, she turned to look at me but instead saw the Lord Himself standing there, right in front of her; His Arms wide open in a welcoming gesture for her to fall into His embrace. I was not there anymore. The sister, with great emotion, fell in Jesus' Arms, and sobbed. She felt His Hair touching her cheek and His Arms around her. It was as if He were telling her, 'Well done My child, for going through these trials for My sake – for welcoming My messenger and defending My Message. Do not worry any more, I am with you and in control of everything.' As she pulled away and looked again, she saw me, and I had no idea what had happened.

'What about the sign of "glitter"?'

This sign was given during our pilgrimage in Turkey, visiting the seven Churches of the Apocalypse. All the pilgrims were gathered in a hotel where most of the speeches were to be given. Having rested in my room before a conference where I was due to speak, I looked at the speech I had prepared on Unity, and went over it again, making a few additions and changes.

When it was my turn to speak to the pilgrims assembled in the conference hall, I read out my speech on Unity. I noticed how attentively everyone listened. After my speech, heading back to my room, I passed a friend who pointed at my face and said that I had glitter all around my mouth and on my cheeks. I paid no attention, and suggested that perhaps it was my lip balm he saw. As soon as I went into my room, however, I noticed there was glitter on the dressing table stool, and looking around I saw glitter of all the colors of the rainbow covering the light beige, wall-to-wall carpet. The glitter multiplied, spreading out to cover all the surfaces – even the phone, the lamps, and the bed sheets. It was just everywhere as well as in heaps at the edges of the walls and in the corners. There was identical, multicolored glitter in the bathroom, and when I looked at my face in the mirror I saw that it was covered with glitter, especially around the mouth! It was as though an Angel had come, dispersing the glitter everywhere, producing the effect of an explosion.

I went out into the corridor and saw more glitter from the left side to the right side of my room door, again giving the impression of a multicolored explosion. I walked along the corridor looking at the doors for signs of glitter, but found none. I called out to the friend who had first seen it on my face, and he came with another friend to see the splendor of my quarters. He was struck not only by the vast quantity but to see so many beautiful colors.

He already knew about the glitter phenomenon as he had seen the gift before on a friend, a very prayerful person, who had also experienced glitter on her face and on everything holy she owned. Her home received glitter daily, but only one color at a time. After research I discovered that this 'glitter' has a name and is called '*escarchas*', which means 'frost' in the Spanish language. Scientists have examined these occurrences and found that it is a living matter, a sort of plasma, and not paper or aluminum. It is something that is not of this world.

The following day I confided in Msgr René Laurentin, who is an expert on mysticism and phenomena, and he simply said: 'It is a Sign given to you from God; God feels glorified by you and wants to tell you that He is with you.'

I heard his words with a sigh of relief, as I had felt unsure of my speech. The Sign was reassuring, telling me that my speech on Unity was what God really wanted me to say, and that He was glorified. The Sign told me that the additions to my speech did not really come from me, but from the Holy Spirit. In such moments one never thinks of taking a picture; however, I had two witnesses who saw the glitter.

'What about the "Shekinah" sign?'

Another phenomenon of God's Glory and Presence is the well-known Shekinah. This usually appears in photographs because of the sensitive eye of the camera. It appears in holy places, on holy people, on religious objects like medallions, crucifixes, and so on, or in assemblies where people gather in the Name of God. It is a form of white mist that looks like a cloud, and one can also call it a pillar of light or of fire. Both names are mentioned in the Old Testament when the Israelites were guided across the desert by the pillar of fire by night, and by a 'cloud', during the daytime.

In today's society, many people believe that we exist for this material world only; a life span that lasts ninety years at best. This is a deception for we are not merely matter but soul and spirit as well, and we are meant for nobility, to live eternally in the spirit world that is Heaven. Yes, we are created for something higher, sovereign, more majestic than this material world that will wear away. My Angel told me one day that nothing lasts where we are, but where he lives, everything lasts forever. He also said that what we call 'the end of our life' is only the beginning of Eternity. So we are not purely matter, or some coincidence of this physical world.

All these signs that are being given have but one goal: to follow the Lord and lead our life into an unceasing prayer. We are all called, without exceptions, to transfigure this earth from its sinfulness into a paradise, thus leading it into glory. Let us fill our earth with glitter, with 'escarchas'. Let us all take the form of our Lord Jesus who sparkles and become light to be absorbed and fade within His Light.

The evening came to an end, but thirsting for more, they asked me if it were possible to meet again in their house.

12

The Day of the Lord

Next day, I met them and as soon as we had sat down they began to ask me in particular about what I experienced when God revealed my soul to me showing me my real self – the way He sees me. I accepted their invitation as I remembered the words that Jesus once pronounced:

> *'I am determined to save this generation by parading My Mercy; so be happy all you who hear the melody of My Voice and have your fill in Me, your God.'*[1]

As soon as we gathered I said:

'Let me put it straight to you: God is Fire …'

Looking at their eyes I noticed they had not grasped what I said. I did not want to mince my words so I added,

'This is called the Day of the Lord. I might as well name it after my own experience the "Day of Choice" or "Baptism of Fire".' It still did not click.

'That Day can come abruptly upon anyone at any time, just as it happened to me. I know others, like myself, who have already experienced this Day and have been through this Fire that razed them to the ground, bringing them to compunction. When you experience it, it is as if God is telling you at that moment,

1 February 12, 2000

'Come! Puny little creature, you who pretend not to see Me. Come now! You've messed up your life enough and My Eyes are too pure to continue to bear the sight of your pagan ways. Just tell Me, where do you think you are going without Me? And how much longer will you continue to rebel against Me? To save you, puny little creature, and get you out of your tomb and revive you, I will, out of My Infinite Mercy, come upon you like someone with a torch entering a dark cave. I will allow Myself to enter your soul to scrutinize every one of your actions; then I will put aflame and burn to the root all that is not Mine.'

Finally, I saw that they had all connected with me, and they asked:

'Are we all going to go through that immaterial Fire?'

'Yes, every one of us will go through the terrible Day of the Lord. No one will escape it. It is a sort of a mini-tribunal before the actual Day of Judgment. And if I were you, I would pray to experience it *now,* while you are still on earth.'

That shocked and confused them, so they asked: 'Why do you say that?'

'Because this Fire reveals and rids you of your innumerable sins. You can call it, "God's Merciful act". God is love, and not less when He reveals Himself as a consuming Fire. It is better to experience this purifying Fire here on earth rather than later in Purgatory. Why? Because your life will become like an unceasing prayer, pleasing to God and it will lessen the amount of time you'll spend in Purgatory after you die, where the soul's suffering is even more intense due to its separation from God.

'God, in His benevolence, showed me in 1986 a vision of the Purgatory I would have gone to had He not come with His Fire. In the vision I saw myself lying on my right side on the ground in a very dark Purgatory, far too weak to sit up – near death. I had the form of a small child around six years old and looked very thin, with barely any hair on my head and the little I had was very short. The 'sky' above me was pitch-black, without a spot of light to be seen. Then I heard myself breathing with difficulty, like an asthmatic. I felt that 'Someone' was standing very near to me in this lonely, dark place. His mere Presence was consoling, because all around me was darkness, emptiness and loneliness. Suddenly He bent over me and lifted me up all the way to His Breast. I could not turn my head to see His Face but I felt immensely loved by this Presence. I saw myself trying to turn my eyes leftwards to catch a glimpse of Him, but could not manage to do so. The white of my eyes were yellowish and I was shocked to see how sick I was! Using what little strength remained in me, and with great effort, my skinny little hand desperately stretched out to grasp His large sleeve and not let go. Immediately, at this pathetic gesture of mine, I felt the Holy One's Heart cry out with pity and sorrow; such pity and such love! Then He carried me ever so gently and tenderly to take me to His House and heal me. Like a watchman, His Eyes never left me, and like a loving mother He raised me. And with His love He healed me.

'Then God said,

> *"I, God, was full of pity for you, to see you so wretched. Daughter, I lifted you to Me and healed your guilt. I wanted you to recognize Me, for I am your Redeemer who loves you. I healed you and blessed you. I unfolded My cloak asking you if you were willing to share it with Me."*[2]

'His words touched me profoundly.'

Those present were speechless. I continued,

'This is why we should ask God to give us the grace to be purified now, seeing our sins the way He sees them so that our soul will be led to repentance. However, this divine Fire performs its actions with different weight according to the person. It depends on what stage you're in spiritually, and your relationship with God. The Day of the Lord can be understood in other terms such as: a sudden "Visitation of the Lord in our life on earth", or a "Baptism of Fire", or a "Baptism of the Holy Spirit". Whether or not we ever see a vision or hear an Angel speak, God will come to each one of us. No one will be spared on that Day, no one will escape. It's in God's "book of rules". While we are experiencing this Fire, we will have to choose – either God will conquer us entirely and bend us to His Will and we will "lose the

---

2 My Angel Daniel, December 2, 1986

battle", or we will continue our rebellion against Him, thinking we can win. To go out of the black obscurity of our soul we need to be shown in our soul what we are carrying.'

Some of my friends who were listening said that they too had undergone similar experiences, but not to such depths of agony. One of my friends blurted out, 'But this is terrifying!' I responded:

'Well, although the Day of the Lord sounds terrifying, one should not fear, because as God put it, we will have unbounded joy when it is over. We will receive the joy of God's Luminous Presence, a better understanding of our Creator, and a more intimate relationship with Him. Above all, this revelation of our soul puts us straight on the right path, and renews our spirit. "*When the renewal takes place*", says the Lord, "*many will be vested with Myself and all the Saints and Angels will give thanks for the gift of My Holy Spirit.*" Therefore, this is a great gift that God offers to us.'

I opened my notebook and read out to them more of what God had told me about this Day and how it will come upon all the earth:

> *'Those who have and are persistently rebelling against Me will taste that Day and all it bears; it will come upon those transgressors as sudden as a thunderbolt, and like a fearful fire they will be turned into human torches.'*[3]

I quickly said,

'Don't be afraid, God is describing how the earth will be set aflame with *a spiritual flame* and our consciousness will be revealed to us as a revelation. This Divine Fire will turn the inflexible heart into a lenient heart on that Day; then the world in agony will become fully aware of its failures and deficiencies, its corruptibility and lawlessness, and not to say the least the infamous rejection of the Lord's Resurrection and of His Omnipresence in our daily life. Heaven will open that Day and those who rejected God, or took the place of God, will be judged severely; while those who kept His precepts and His Laws based on love will not be tested by fire, since God is indeed their God, and

3 June 1, 2002

they have acknowledged Him as the principal of their life. They have already been tested …

'People ask me, "When is this Day coming?" This Day has started and is under way, since many people have already experienced this immaterial Fire. The less spiritual people are, the more they will have to suffer in their soul; it all depends on the condition of one's soul. But let me share with you what God said:

> *"Alas for those who centered their lives on material things, when My Day comes; My appearance will be Fire. Already My Footsteps are heard and My Footprints seen by many; when I reveal Myself to those who did not acknowledge Me, when in these times of grace I presented Myself as Mercy and as a Lamp, I will reveal Myself then as a consuming Fire. Why, did anyone believe I would pass by unnoticed? And do you still believe that the Master will pass you by without any retribution? It is, therefore, good to repent daily."*[4]

'Our spirit in its sinfulness will shrivel with fear when this inner revelation of soul is exposed in our consciousness and especially when we recognize that it comes from God.'

I saw again how they were resisting this Message, so I asked, 'But don't you want to know the truth about your soul?'

One of them managed to say: 'Yes, of course. But it's frightening. Can you explain more about the positive side of it?'

'Yes! While this is going on, God will be exuding His Fragrance on your soul, purifying it and embellishing it, and the scales covering your eyes will fall off. You will be given the grace, which is a tremendous thing, to look at your real self. God's Fire will reduce you to nothing in your dismay, but God assures us that we shouldn't fear because this process puts us by God's side and directs our soul so that it no longer ventures here and there aimlessly. This is wonderful.'

'Will any kind of warning be given before this happens?' they asked.

'No. The Lord will come like a "thief in the night" without any forewarning. Let me read you what the Lord said:

4 June 1, 2002

> *"When the voice of the bird is silenced and song notes are still, know that I will call in this silence all your hidden deeds, good or bad, to judgment."*'[5]

I continued my explanation:

'After all these years journeying with God, something beautiful welled up inside me and I'm sure that this was after I experienced the Day of the Lord. I was alone and deep in thought, thinking of God, when He made me realize in an instant and without any preparation or warning that I was created just for Him and that I did not even belong to my own family, not even to myself!

'I was free! Free from everything, free of the world. I cannot adequately describe how I came to be in this state of spirit. In a flash, the Lord made me understand that except for God I belonged to no one: I was His. At the moment I realized this, suddenly the conviction came of being a total stranger on earth and quite different, unique. I must admit that this feeling of total detachment and dispassion gave me great joy and at the same time a feeling of warmth and freedom mingled with security within me. If I believed in UFOs I would have said, "I am an alien and I don't belong among humans nor am I from this planet, for I feel different and yet no one suspects it." I look quite ordinary, a plain housewife on the outside, but within in some really odd way it was as if God had created me and trained me for one purpose only: *to lend* me out to the world, to mingle among them and be His Echo, echoing His Words from the Love Hymn He dictated to me naming it Himself "True Life in God". In short: I am God's child, trained by Him and sent as an unsuspected "secret agent" on earth to look after His Interests.

'My purpose of my being created is to be a witness and work for the spreading of His Kingdom. Engraved in me is one objective: to serve God and offer myself as an oblation. He planned this mission long before He created me; He told me so. He created me at this specific time in history, for this specific mission. Each one of us has a mission on earth.'

One of my friends said: 'We are not all Mother Teresa you know and we cannot come to her level. I am just a housewife, what's my mission?'

---

5 September 13, 2002

'To be a good housewife and take care of what God has given you. He always shows everyone what services one has to do in this life, but whatever we do, we must do it with love. We are not all the same. Everyone is different. Take as example glasses of different sizes. So long as each glass is filled to the brim with love and goodness, no matter the size of glass, God is glorified. Also the more graces one receives from God, all the more one has to give back to God.

'We must discover the inestimable treasures that overshadow every earthly power. This Treasure that glitters with amazing Light is right in front of our eyes and at everyone's reach, available to us all without exception. God is Fire, but Light as well. I knew that my mind would not have been able to ascend and reach God even if I had tried hard, but through grace I was lifted to discover God's mysteries.

'My faith was revived and preceded the love of God, which by its value is a pearl beyond compare. This Light enables our spiritual eyes to see the Treasure He places before us, and when we do, we'll trade everything we have to possess It. It is the "Pearl of great price" – beyond compare. But to obtain it, one has to undergo "the Day of the Lord."'

The evening came to a close. Many of them were cut to the heart. Some of them went on to become witnesses and have created ecumenical prayer groups associated with the Messages.

13

The Spiritual Battle

One of the most important things to understand in the spiritual life is spiritual warfare. Spiritual warfare is the battle between Good and Evil and the battlefield is us. It is warfare not against flesh and blood but against principalities and powers. In the spiritual battle of our times we are *all* participants.

Let us hear what Jesus said to me one day: *'Today there is a great battle going on.'*[1]

Light and Darkness have nothing in common. Good Angels are not allies of rebel angels (demons). There are invisible powers in Heaven that were created, which we call Thrones, Dominations, Sovereignties, and Powers. There are presences of malevolent forces and of Good forces that surround us. The army of the Good Angels that God provides is far greater in numbers and much more powerful than the army of the dark forces.

Spirits are immortal. We have learned that a great multitude of angels fell, and later, man's soul fell as well and their fall brought misery, sin, and death. Had it not been for God who, under His command ordered light and light began, the whole of the spiritual world would have been in shambles, sucked away as asteroids are sucked into and disappear in a black hole.

Among the powers of evil, Satan is above all other demons. When he feels he is losing a soul he will take any action to paralyze it. He will not hesitate to use people and situations, even all the laws of nature

1 November 21, 1988

against the one he fears he will be losing. He will turn everything against this soul, especially when he senses that this soul will turn against him one day and become his enemy, destroying his plans.

I came to realize these evil forces want the destruction of both our body and more importantly, the destruction of our soul. The demons would love to see us spend eternity in Hell with them, and suffer as they suffer. They would drive many people to fall into apostasy and deny God. They would do everything they can to damage God's creation. The wars, the crimes, the hatred of one nation against the other, the disruption of families and friendships, the abortions, the disagreements and ongoing division of the Churches, all these things are in some way manipulations of demons.

The demons are angry with God that He loves us. They are angry with anyone who becomes a collaborator with God and threatens their evil plans. They are angry when God shows compassion and mercy to save us. They are jealous when we claim our rightful place as children of God. They get infuriated with despair when they realize that they are going to lose the battle in the end, but in the meantime they continue ranting with rage and do everything possible to destroy all that God loves and values. It is a battle with the dark spiritual forces that desire to infest and corrupt our minds and lead us to do evil so that we will join those demons in Hell.

Hell was created after the fall of the angels, after the battle between Saint Michael and Lucifer with his cohorts. That is their domain. We have to believe in the spirit world; we have to believe in the supernatural, because many things that we can't see physically really do exist. Heaven and Hell exist.

The forces of Darkness are increasing and covering many nations like mist, and yet we cannot say that we were not given signs of this warfare! The majority of people avoid discussing these matters, preferring to change the subject or close their ears. If they are afraid, it means they believe but do not want to approach the issue for various reasons. And yet, if we open our spiritual eye, we will see the great army of God's Angels encircling this fiery battlefield of the rebel angels, just as I have seen them in the vision that God has given me.

We are all participants in this battle and the weapon given for us to use is *prayer* in order to overcome our enemies and end up triumphant. When we are a sincerely prayerful person we are automatically on God's side and we should not fear, even in our weaknesses, because God's power is at its best in our weakness.

My mission given to me by Christ is Unity of the Churches, a task far beyond my capacity. Yet God uses our incapacity and weakness to show the power of His Arm, for it is in our weakness and our dependence on God that we can be strong.

Jesus said to me:

> *'I have given you the virtue of fortitude to be the principle of all your other virtues in you; since I was preparing your soul for this battle of your times, where good is deformed into evil.'*[2]

> *'I am reminding you little grain that you are fighting in the same battle as all my prophets fought. Gales can blow on you, floods can rise to drown you, but nothing of these will overcome you, for I am with you and in my good care to withstand your frailty.'*[3]

> *'Anyone who defends faithfully the Church and witnesses, are for Us [the Holy Trinity], like living torches because their words flare in the darkness of the world; I give them a warrior's heart, to fight the good fight of faith and justice and join in this spiritual battle of your times My Archangels, Michael and Raphael, who are predominant in strength and valiant Warriors of Justice, observing through My Light every aspect of human behavior.'*[4]

God knows how frail we are. He sees our sincere efforts, that we are trying to 'fight the good fight', trying to please Him, and yet not achieving our goals. He can take over. The Lord wants to come in and 'save the day' because that will remind us that it's His power, not our own.

---

2 June 22, 1998

3 June 21, 1999

4 June 22, 1998

This life is a spiritual battle, and in that battle, we will be wounded at times. It may even look as if we've lost the battle, and we're lying dead on the battlefield. But then Jesus asks us to turn to His Mother, the Virgin Mary for consolation. These are His words:

> *'Today in these end times, where the battle is raging on our two Hearts [Jesus' and Mary's] and on Our children who witness the Truth, I tell you: run to your Blessed Mother, who, like a hen who hides her chicks under Her wings, will hide you, too, under Her Mantle.'*[5]

> *'If the world inflicts on you impressive wounds, turn to your Mother and She will dress your wounds with Her Maternal Love and Affection.'*[6]

I remember when I could not manage to fulfill something He asked for, despite my best efforts. I was so disappointed, but then ever so swiftly, Jesus appeared and told me in a very fatherly way, *'Do not worry, you are only learning now, and I am pleased with your efforts, because I saw that you are trying.'*

At the same time, when we make a promise to Him, we must follow through. Our willingness at the beginning and the good intentions of words should be followed through by actions, so they do not become empty words. The Lord is honored when we remain consistent and faithful to the bitter end.

As I began to receive more and more invitations to witness I remembered how God had told me that '*full you shall be many*'. This was to fulfill what God said in the beginning. He had foretold me enigmatically these words that meant that in the fullness of His Holy Spirit in me, many will be converted through my echoing the Words of God. He foretold me that He will be sending me across the seas to every nation with His Message, covering the globe and to people who never even knew Him. And so it happened, and I began to travel to many nations, running like a sprint athlete, like a globetrotter. Some received me with open arms and received the Word of God with an

5 April 3, 1996

6 December 13, 1992

open heart. At other times I was in for a battle from the minute I stepped off the airplane. *'Terror assails them [the demons] in broad daylight at the sound of the Holy Spirit'*, said the Lord to me one day. But that was in the 'package deal'.

Now I was trained to be strong and my invincible weapons were a Rosary in one hand and a Cross in the other. On January 7, 2002 Jesus said to me:

> *'In My gracious condescension I deigned to choose you, train you and form you into an athlete; now I have the satisfaction of seeing you eager to please Me by willing to go into the battlefield.'*

We are all in this race one way or another and even more when we are engaged to work for God. Working for God is to be enrolled in a battlefield and *placed in the front line.*

We must begin our race well and God will encourage us to finish the race by completing whatever mission He has given us and be triumphant, winning the prize so that we can say just like Saint Paul: *'I have fought the good fight and I have finished the race, I have kept the faith.'*[7] Therefore, God can train us to be strong in that battlefield and not run aimlessly, like headless chickens, but with the intent to win, saying what Saint Paul said: *'That is how I run, intent on winning; that is how I fight, not beating the air.'*[8]

At one point, I was invited to speak in Puerto Rico. The Bishop had decided to organize the meeting on what is known as the Holy Mountain where there is also a church. Seven thousand people gathered on the mountaintop. However, not all his clergy were in favor of his invitation to me, and this created a division between the Bishop and the clergy. Throughout the preparation for the meeting, a priest in his diocese constantly opposed the poor Bishop and my coming. He said that all other Christians outside the Roman Catholic Church are schismatic, so by being Greek Orthodox, I was a schismatic and it was outrageous that a Catholic bishop would invite me to speak. Prejudice

---

7 Timothy 4: 7

8 1 Corinthians 9: 26

and pride can blind us; they can often make us close our hearts and fuel evil and conflict where God had intended good.

When I arrived at the meeting, I saw this priest sitting in the front with a small tape recorder. I felt sorry for him because he was sweating and flushed from having climbed the steep mountain to get there. While I was in the middle of my speech, talking about the Holy Spirit, I suddenly noticed that the people became very excited and were no longer looking at me, but at the sun. To many, it appeared as if the sun started to spin with different colors around it. I turned around and saw this miracle, but only for a short while, and then returned to reading out the Message of Jesus. The priest also saw the 'miracle of the sun', and yet his response was to criticize me because I had not given the sign enough attention, and had instead continued to read out the Message.

This extraordinary sign in the sun was expressed so powerfully and so majestically that it produced reverence for the Message I was reading. It left everyone in awe. Those who previously had doubts came to tell me that not only did they see the sun spinning, but also had seen Christ's Holy Face in the sky as well as on mine. The Holy Face of Christ that was superimposed on mine was sad and wearing the crown of thorns, with blood streaming down over His entire Face.

Now, the devil can imitate God's actions, but he cannot counterfeit the glory and the majesty of one of God's holy manifestations.

Nonetheless, following this event, the priest became my greatest persecutor in Puerto Rico, calling me in newsletters a witch and a satanist.

This was one of those many battles where I had a chance to follow through on my lofty commitments to follow and serve God. But of course, like most of us, I approached God and complained:

'I have become an object of derision … How many more malicious things will they say about me? Even in return for my friendship, they denounce me, though all I have done was Your will not mine. Will You not defend my innocence?'

God responded with these words:

'Do not fear for I am near you. Allow these things to happen, for with this sacrifice I obtain souls who are on the road to perdition; ah, Vassula ... one day I will show you the vast multitude of souls I saved through the wounds your detractors imposed on you and through your acts of reparation ... My Love for souls passes every possible understanding and I tell you, My thirst for wretched souls is great! How can I then remain indifferent? How? When hordes of nations fall into apostasy and rebellion? Today's rebellion is even greater than the Great Rebellion known in the past;[9] does a shepherd abandon his flock? I am your Shepherd and I love My little flock.'[10]

We humans don't enjoy the trials we undergo. Yet, there are always good reasons for our trials, even if we can't see them. I try to always remind myself that everything I endure in this spiritual battle can be used by God's salvation plan and for my own good. When we belong to God, He can use our crosses as 'celestial works' to save others who reject Him and are bound for damnation. Or, He can use our trials for our own sanctification. In either case, He will always use them for good.

The same is true for our failures. On January 7, 2002, Jesus reminded me:

'As for your failures and your lacking, I filled where you lacked, and in My exuberant love I have for you, it obliges Me to take care Myself where you had failed Me. In My fatherly Mercy I looked upon all your negligence as a father would look upon the negligence of his own little child: with compassion and ever so ready to help out with tenderness, whispering soft words of love so as not to frighten you away while showing you once more how I care for you and for your own progress.

---

9 Psalms 95: 8–11

10 June 26, 1994

> *'As for the afflictions you suffer for the sake of My Church and for My Sake, My sister, My cathedral, do not despair; with one single of My glances I rebuild what has fallen.*
>
> *'... When I showed My Cup to you, you rose and said: "Jesus, allow me to drink from It, offering You thus everything that may bring You consolation;" and I, touched and delighted with your offer reclined on you and embraced you; I was embracing in My Arms a little daffodil; hardly born and hardly out of her ill-health, yet all heart.*
>
> *'... When I saw you running towards the Altar decisively with determination, a great sound was heard from heaven, singing: "Alleluia! Glory to our Lord who conquered her!" after this, I lifted the Cup to your lips ordering you to taste It only but not empty Its contents; I said: "bring My people to Me and put them alltogether around one Altar; preach the obedience of faith to all nations in honor of My Name; show them how absurd it is to remain divided; I will always be at your side."'*

And I, encouraged and filled with His love, answered Him,

'Lord, in the folly of Your Love, You have sought me and found me ... When in difficulties on all sides You lifted my soul to soar the skies with You and relieve me from the forked tongues ... They knocked me down several times, but never managed to kill my spirit and never will because You are my Refuge.'

God also showed me how the words from the book of Daniel, the prophet, are so relevant to our times. Daniel saw in a vision a man dressed in linen, who said to him that in the End of Times many will be cleansed, made white and purged; that the wicked will go on doing wrong; the wicked will never understand; the learned will understand.

These events will all happen at the End of Times and the sign will be that *'the Perpetual Sacrifice will be abolished and the disastrous Abomination of the desolation erected in the Holy Place.'*[11] To make me better understand what that means, God showed me how many churches and Cathedrals were being sold for lack of priests, lack of

11 Daniel 11: 31

funds and lack of attendance by the faithful. These churches are being turned into expensive restaurants, hotels, cafeterias, and casinos.

In these former Cathedrals, where sacred rites were performed and God was worshipped, the Holy Altars have been converted into bars and billiard tables. The Holy Altar was the Holy Place where the priests once performed the Consecration, the Perpetual Sacrifice of Christ in which bread and wine are transubstantiated into the real Body and the real Blood of Jesus Christ.

To help me fully understand the grave situation of the Church, one night God gave me a dream. In it I saw how Pope John Paul II[12] suffered because of this general apostasy and rebellion. I was shown Rome and I found myself standing in St Peter's Basilica for the first time. The Basilica was empty. I looked around and saw the marble floor – it was beautiful. Then I saw a frightening scene: snakes were slithering on the great Altar. It was neglected and the cloth covering it was dusty, with cobwebs here and there. The Pope was sitting alone on his throne, his right arm placed on the arm of the throne, with his hand holding his temple, resting his head. He was as if in thought, but in reality he was tormented. Jesus made me understand that he was alone, for so many of his own were contradicting him and rebelling against him. I felt very sad for him.

And then, God gave me a Message for the Pope. I mumbled: 'Use all of me as atonement for Your Sacred Intentions.' The major problem was, I thought, 'How on earth am I supposed to go to the Vatican and just hand in that Message to the Pope?' I've always said and I still say, that it is easier to enter the Courts of Heaven than to enter the Vatican courts! It's much easier to meet God and talk to Him than to meet and talk to any of the Vatican prelates, let alone the Pope! But I left everything in God's Hands and trusted He would show me the way. More than ever, I simply had to obey. So off to Rome I went, without any appointment or any clue as to how I would meet the Pope. I traveled by train with a priest friend, and we eventually arrived in Rome, the 'Eternal City'.

Visiting Rome is an awesome experience. Everywhere you look there are the remnants of the great Roman Empire, and the monuments its rulers built to survive their short lives. Beyond these ruins, there is one

12 Pope from 1978 to 2005

structure that is still standing, built in layers, over centuries, upon the bones of the great Apostle: St Peter's Basilica. When you arrive at St Peter's, the 'front door' of the Vatican, you can't help but marvel at the sight. The genius of some of the greatest and most gifted artisans in history – including Michelangelo – surrounds you. Everything was designed as a tribute to God, a symphony in marble, granite, and awe-inspiring art. The builders sought to display the glory of God – and it shows. Standing inside the Basilica, you are little more than a speck in the midst of its grandeur. Yet there I was, called by the Creator, trying to figure out how to penetrate it in order to meet the Pope.

We knew that every Wednesday the Pope received the faithful in a general audience held in the big Hall of the Vatican. Admission was by ticket only, so we rushed to the Vatican Office and managed to obtain two tickets. The Office gives out these tickets randomly, showing the enclosure and the line number where you are to sit. No one can make a special request; one is obliged to go to the area shown on the ticket. Once inside, I began to see God's plan in motion, as our tickets put us in a section right next to the enclosure fence on the aisle where the Pope would pass! Had I been sitting elsewhere, I would not have been able to accomplish the crazy thing I was about to do.

The hall was packed with four thousand people from all over the world. Everyone was jubilant, singing loudly and excitedly anticipating the Pope's arrival. I was calm, but very happy that I had gotten this far. Now, my *mission impossible* had to go into action.

When the Pope walked in, the cheers were even louder. He gave his speech, and when it ended he started to walk slowly up the large aisle, first along my side of the aisle, and then he intended to go to the opposite side, and walk down again, blessing the people as he passed by, but never stopping, as that was against protocol. As he came closer to me, I took out a piece of paper on which I had written the Message. The Pope stopped right in front of me, facing me, blessing the crowd behind me, along my row. I reached out and slipped the Message into his hand. The Pope must have felt something was being slipped into his hand, but as I'm sure that happens to him quite often, he managed to place it back in my hand, all without any change of expression, simply continuing to smile before calmly walking away.

I felt my heart fall with a thud to the floor. 'I failed, I failed!' I thought. Then something extraordinary happened. Right behind me was a Polish priest, standing on his chair, almost leaning over me, who was calling joyfully to the Pope, non-stop. The Pope turned his head to look at him and smiled, recognizing this was a fellow Polish countryman. Then the Pope walked back, something he never does, and stood precisely in front of me again, looking up towards the priest. I stretched out my hand to the wide sash around the Pope's waist, and easily tucked the Message inside. Just as I did so, the priest, stretching precariously over me, held my arm to keep his balance, and unwittingly guided my hand to the Pope's sash. I then noticed that the tip of the Message was visible and easily noticeable, so I stretched out my hand again and tapped the paper well behind the sash. I knew that later on when the Pope went to his quarters and removed his robe, the Message would drop from the sash and he would read it.

Amazingly, in spite of all the security and photographers along with the Archbishops accompanying him, no one noticed what I had done. The Vatican photographer snapped a picture at that very moment. I sighed with relief: Mission accomplished. The priest accompanying me, even though he knew what I was up to, had been so excited to see the Pope, that he never noticed a thing either. Once outside in St Peter's Square, he was afraid to even ask me if I had succeeded. When I told him what had happened, he was surprised to the point that a tsunami hitting him there and then would have had less of an impact on him than my news. It was such a shock that he was not far from fainting right in the middle of St Peter's Square.

Sometime after my first Pope encounter, on January 6, 1994, the feast of Epiphany, I had another dream with Pope John Paul II. I saw the Pope very clearly in his white robes. He was standing opposite me, looking at me. It seemed as though we knew each other well. Between us stood a plastic, cream-colored dining table and I understood that the plastic table represented simplicity. I looked at his white robes, studying them. There was no exchange of words, but we both felt comfortable with each other, and he then sat down at my table, waiting for his meal. Feeling excited, I turned around to my right to open a cupboard and take out a dish containing a dessert I had prepared for him.

I sat opposite him and watched as he ate the dessert, obviously enjoying it. Then, having eaten, he got up to leave. I hurried to accompany him to the door, but as I went by his right side I saw that he was using a walking cane. The cane was also a creamy white color and not made of expensive wood but of some other, plastic-like material, formed to look like bamboo. Using the cane he started to walk towards the door and I noticed that even when using the walking stick he had difficulty in walking. (This was just before the Pope started using a cane in real life.)

For a moment I thought he might fall, so without hesitating and without permission, I grabbed his right arm and pulled it around my neck and shoulders to support him. He did not object and accepted my help. Then I placed my left arm around his waist so as to lift him as much as possible onto my left side, bearing his weight on my back. In this way his feet almost left the floor. When I placed my left arm around him, I felt his ribs. I was astonished at how thin he was. One could not tell how emaciated he was by looking at him in his loose vestments. The Pope made no objection to my assistance during the whole time I was carrying him on my back.

In my thoughts, following the dream the Lord allowed me to understand it: the Pope represented the Church. Not long before this vision, a priest friend of mine had met the Pope and had given him one of the books containing the Messages. Later another priest saw the book in the Pope's private chapel. The dessert I now saw the Pope eating in my dream represented the Messages of God. When he ate the dessert, it meant that he had read the Messages and that he appreciated them, and that they are a good means of evangelization.

Then the Lord made me also understand that the image of the Pope walking with a cane, needing help, and emaciated under his vestments represented how alarmingly weak and vulnerable the Church has become, largely due to the divisions within it that spread global apostasy. Though it may look healthy on the outside, the Church had become weakened from within, in need of spiritual nourishment. Carrying the Pope on my back meant that my mission was to help support the Church *through the Messages and my witnessing,* and not just the institutional Church, but all people of faith who make up the mystical body of the Church.

This was to confirm as well the Message that Christ gave to me one day, *'I need to consolidate My Church.'* He would not have said this if the Church was strong and healthy.

Prayers are needed to conquer the divisions, bind the mouth of Moloch, the god of human sacrifice, end up apostasy, the wars, terrorism, and the crimes etc. and hang on to the Lord. Although God is invisible, He is still with us and among us. When God will reveal Himself in the end in all His glory, He will defeat the devil and his entire cohort in His time. In the meantime, people should learn to ask the Mighty Warrior of all times: Saint Michael the Archangel for protection, a prayer that the devil conveniently hushed down for years. This is what we should pray daily:

Saint Michael the Archangel defend us in this battle,

Be our safeguard against the wickedness and the snares of the devil

May God rebuke him, we humbly pray

And do thou O Prince of the heavenly host

By the power of God cast into Hell Satan and all the other evil spirits

who prowl through the world seeking the ruin of souls. Amen.

14

Prophecies

There are not only personal, spiritual battles we must face in life. There are also the physical challenges of the world. And in our age, these challenges will soon increase for all of us. It has been revealed to me, and many others, that the earth will suffer because of our sins. God's messengers, and God Himself, have been warning us, imploring us to change before it's too late. His aim is to bring us back to our senses, spurring us to make the right decisions so that we can avoid, or at least lessen, the future calamities. These prophetic announcements of future events, declared by God, usually reassure the faithful and never omit to provide us with a solution, no matter how serious the events foretold.

During all these years of my mission, the solutions God has offered through the Messages have always been the same: to each of us individually: 'change your hearts and repent'; to the Church: 'reconcile and overcome your divisions, as these divisions have weakened you and are a scandal; and stop aiming venomous arrows at one another, heaping divine justice upon you.'

When the Messages contain warnings – that is, when they announce something that is yet to come – it is because the warning is conditional and the future events can be modified *based on our response*. The book of Jonah in the Bible is a great example of this. God warned the people of Nineveh, through the prophet Jonah, that calamity would soon come upon them if they did not change their ways. The people heeded the warning, repenting and fasting, and the calamity was averted.

Throughout these recent years, God has shown me future disasters that our sins will bring upon us, if we don't change our ways. Among other things, I was warned symbolically about the attack on New York's World Trade Center (the Twin Towers) on 9/11, as well as the first Asian tsunami. I will explain that in more detail later. But far more serious than either of those tragedies is the 'Chastisement of Fire' that God has shown me and will come upon the earth. The Fire will come like a hurricane of fire and will destroy three-fourths of the earth.

Let me first explain prophecy in general.

Prophecy has always existed, both before the coming of Christ, and since His coming. The Bible tells us that Elijah the prophet, who lived during the Old Testament times, long before Christ, never died, at least not in the sense that the rest of us do. Instead, he was taken up in a chariot of fire, while his protégé, Elisha, looked on in amazement. This unique privilege God granted to the prophet can be interpreted as a symbol that *the prophetic ministry of Elijah will never die.* There is a sense among some religious people that all prophecy ended with the Bible, which was completed almost 2,000 years ago. But nowhere in the Bible does it say that God cannot give prophetic ministries when He chooses, and to whom He chooses – and He has done so through the ages. The important thing is that new prophecies cannot contradict anything in the Bible, as that would be a sign that such messages are not 'of God'.

The Israelite prophets of the Old Testament frequently used the phrase, 'Thus says the Lord …' In the Messages I've received, one will similarly see the phrase 'Hear Me …' Just as in the style of the old prophets, God expresses Himself in the first person in a poetic way, with authority and majesty, but also with tenderness.

The prophetic gift played a major role in the history of the Church, and in the lives of those to whom the prophecies are targeted. This gift, which is listed in the Bible as one of major gifts of the Holy Spirit, has also had a tendency to provoke negative reactions on the part of the Church hierarchy, since God many times sends Messages reprimanding them for their negligence in carrying out their God-given duties. Some Church leaders will insist that the Holy Spirit's guidance, and admonitions, can only come through them – the consecrated or elected. They flatly reject any voices of correction that come from outside those ranks. The prophets nonetheless remain a voice within the Church for the benefit of the Church. History has shown that God can and does use lesser instruments as well – simple, even 'ignorant', people, like Joan of Arc, who have little theological training of any kind.

The prophet's task is to rebuke without mincing his words when told by God to do so. Otherwise if he does not he will also be held accountable. When there is despair among people the prophet is told to go and console them with kindness, giving them hope. When the people of the Church are in sin – as we have seen through things like the abuse scandals – God strongly rebukes these perverted acts but at the same time intervenes to correct them. He will correct the Church but will never attack it or demolish it. God will warn the Church so that it avoids destruction. The Bible makes it clear, the evil will never overcome the Church: *'The gates of hell will not prevail against it.'*[1]

The Lord Himself explained the role of the prophet in His Message of February 12, 2000:

> *'I have taught My prophets to contemplate Me in My Holiness allowing them and giving them access to My Nobility to rejoice in My direct Presence and taste My sweetness. Therefore, the only theology and, I would strongly add, the only true theology is the contemplation of Me, your God and a foretaste of the Beatific Vision; this is the true and holy theology. It is not the learned theologian who shifts his papers with his theology that turns him into a prophet to prophecy, but those I, Myself, anointed with the unction of My Love, embedding them well within My Heart to reach the interior Divine and extraordinary inspirations that lie in My Heart, to be pronounced like fire to My people ...*
>
> *'I had since eternity foreseen this apostasy in the Church as well, but I also have foreseen My Salvific plan in you, where*

1 Matthew 16: 18

I would descend from My Throne and address you in divine poetry My Love Theme and reveal to you and through you to others My loving intercession through My Infinite Mercy ...'

God can use anyone He wants to serve as a prophet. In 1917, during World War I, the Lord sent the Virgin Mary to Fatima, a village in Portugal, where she appeared to three poor illiterate children. She told them that if the world did not repent and return to God, a Second World War would come, worse than the first, and that Russia would spread her errors all over the world. The Church and the people of the world were supposed to take these warnings seriously and act immediately. But instead the children of Fatima were mistreated and the prophecies of the Virgin Mary were neglected. Sadly, everything told by Mary to the children came true. World War II started twenty-three years after the apparitions at Fatima and led to the deaths of millions of people, and starting with the Bolshevik Revolution in 1917, the same year as the apparitions, Communism spread all over the world, enslaving and killing millions of people.

In the 1980s, when the Soviet Union and the other Communist countries were still at the height of their power, no one could have predicted that Communism in Europe would soon fall into ashes. But on January 4, 1988 I heard Christ calling my name urgently and from the tone of His Voice I knew He was afflicted. I rushed to get a pencil to write. He said:

'I have one of My beloved daughters lying dead! A sister of yours!'

I understood why the Lord called the Soviet Union, my 'sister', because its inhabitants are also primarily Orthodox Christians like me.

'Who's lying dead, Lord?'

'My well-beloved daughter Russia!'

Notice here that the Lord called her by her proper name. Then, as though He was in a rush, the Lord said,

'Come! Come and I will show her to you!'

He took my spirit into a vision. I saw myself standing in a vast wilderness at the edge of a desert. He pointed with His Finger at a woman, who laid dead a couple of meters ahead of me in the desert under a scorching sun. Her body was emaciated from tyranny, and she seemed abandoned even at her death. In a vision one feels everything and everything becomes alive. When I saw her state and how sorrowful our Lord was I felt so sorry that I burst into tears. '*O, do not weep, I will resurrect her for My Glory. I will revive her as I revived Lazarus!*' the Lord exclaimed.

Then, in metaphorical terms, the Lord explained to me that during these years of Communism in Russia and other countries, they had burnt His Houses (the churches) and become atheists. Then He said that I should stop weeping because He was near Russia right now with His Hand on her heart to warm her heart, resurrect her and *transfigure* her so that she may glorify Him. Not long after that, we heard that Communism in Russia had died: this prophecy came true during the Orthodox Feast of the *Transfiguration* in August, 1991, with the dissolution of the Soviet Union, which formally dissolved on December 25, 1991, the commemoration of Christ's Birth!

Had we listened to God's warnings through the Virgin Mary in 1917, we could have avoided a tremendous amount of suffering. And the same is true now as He continues to warn us and call us to repentance.

I had received many more prophecies about Russia's return to God, but what struck me most were the prophecies of how she will rise to be the country that will glorify God more than anyone else and that she would be the head of many nations. The Lord strongly expressed Himself of her powerful revival with words such as, '*Russia you will live!*' These last prophecies, showing that Russia will defend Christianity in a most powerful way, are yet to come. Here is a short excerpt from a Message given on December 13, 1993:

> *'I tell you, your sister Russia will be the head of many nations and will glorify me in the end … I will place her shepherds at the head of innumerable nations.'*

The first prophecy of the Chastisement of Fire was given to me in a vision on September 1, 1987. I was called by God:

> *'Vassula, I will give you a vision lifting you to Me. I will show you how Heaven will appear.'*

The sky was shown to me. It looked as any night with its stars. Then it changed. Instead of the stars, something else started to appear, something menacing. I was seeing what resembled spots of paint, like on a painter's palette, but one color was dominating the others, surpassing all others and in command. It was red, crimson red and it grew, getting thicker, like yeast pouring on us from above. This prophecy has yet to come: we are given warnings and time to change our heart. The red thick 'paint' could have been lava or fire.

This prophecy was expanded with further explanations from God, which you will read below. This is what the Lord said:

> *'I have, since the beginning of times, loved My creation, but I created My creation to love Me too and recognize Me as their God; ... since the beginning of times, I have shown My Love to mankind, but I have also shown My Justice too; ... The world has incessantly been offending Me and I, for My part, have incessantly been reminding them of My existence and of how I love them, My Chalice of Justice is full, creation! ... My cries resound and shake the entire heavens leaving all My angels trembling for what has to come, I am a God of Justice and My Eyes have grown weary watching hypocrisy, atheism, immorality; My creation has become, in its decadence, a replica of what Sodom was; I will thunder you with My Justice as I have thundered the Sodomites; repent, creation, before I come.'*

The Lord out of His Mercy does not like to punish us; this is why He comes to bring us back to health. The question is, do we even know we need a doctor? Do we even recognize and appreciate His Mercy?

On May 4, 1988, God gave me another vision of the Chastisement of Fire, which made me tremble. I saw myself standing outdoors, when all of a sudden a strong, fiery, poisonous and deadly wind blew over nature. When it passed over the trees they withered instantly and dried up, burnt. It was like a hurricane of fire, leaving sorrow and death in its wake. People were running, trying to inhale fresh air, but as they breathed the air they were instantly scorched within themselves, as if they had swallowed fire. Jesus told me:

> *'The Time is imminent, ever so imminent! O come! My beloved ones! Come to Me! I am the Way, the Truth and the Life; come to me now when there is still time; when the grass is still green and the flowers still blooming on the trees; O come! I love you exceedingly! I have loved you always in spite of your wickedness and your evil doings ... ah, the time is almost over, what is to come is so very near you!'*

Again in the year 1994, December 18:

> *'My Church will break into joyful cries one day, because in My everlasting love I will end this Apostasy quicker than foreseen; ... the worst has to come, nothing can be brought forth all at once; My Father will reveal His Mighty Hand to the poor, but to the apostates and to the Rebel, a hurricane of fire from the east will scorch them because of all the filthy things they have done ... the culprit will die for his guilt; if he converts before My Day and restores what he has been destroying and acknowledge his sin, I will forgive him and he will live and not die; this is My Law thrice Holy.'*

The Lord has spoken of this Fire so many times, warning us, and every time people ask me whether He is speaking in metaphors or literally. They ask me if this Fire will be atomic or caused naturally – perhaps by an asteroid, for example. I respond:

'I don't know. All that I know is that it is a real fire the Lord is talking about; He even named it, "*hurricane of fire*". It is as though the atmosphere will ignite and He made me see it twice in visions. I have written all these prophecies in the "True Life in God" Messages.'

On September 11, 1991, Jesus gave me an astounding prophecy, which would later prove to be tragic for the United States of America. It was exactly ten years to the day before the great disaster of the Twin

Towers in the USA. In the Message, our Lord was very displeased with humanity. With a heavy Heart, He asked me to write down this Message,

> *'My Eyes look down at the world of today, searching nation after nation, scanning soul after soul for some warmth, for some generosity and for some love, but very few enjoy My favor. Very few bother to live a holy life and the days are fleeing and the hours are now counted before the great retribution.'*

Then Jesus suddenly changed His tone and gravely said:

> *'The earth will shiver and shake and every evil built into Towers will collapse into a heap of rubble and be buried in the dust of sin! Above, the Heavens will shake and the foundations of the earth will rock!'*

Exactly ten years to the day later, on September 11, 2001, the towers fell in New York as a result of the greatest terrorist attack in American history.

The horrific, apocalyptic experience of 9/11 shocked the world. It drove the people of America to their knees. For a while churches were packed and people turned to God. The people of New York City, who have the reputation of being gruff and high-strung due to the stress of city life, suddenly slowed down, became kinder toward each other, and focused on what matters most in life.

But soon, the shock wore off. And instead of truly turning to God and repenting, the world became worse than before. Instead of understanding that these tragedies come upon us because of our own sins, the world continued to follow the devil's way, rather than God's.

On December 26, 2004, a tsunami hit Sumatra and other countries of the Indian Ocean, killing over 230,000 people from many nations. Jesus had also given me prophecies about this disaster, warning me four different times in the years before it happened.

The first prophecy of the tsunami came on September 10, 1987.

This is what I wrote in my notebook:

'Suddenly Jesus reminded me of a dream I had last night and had forgotten. It was the vision I saw lately, but it appeared worse in my dream. The Lord said:

> *"Listen, I have let you see the vision in your sleep, to make you feel it. No, there is no escape!"'*

I wrote:

'I remember when I saw it coming like a gigantic wave. I tried to run and hide, knowing it was impossible.'

I asked our Lord, 'But why do this, if You Love us? Why?'

He answered, *'I am known as a God of Love, as well as a God of Justice.'*

I asked, 'What can we do to stop this?'

God answered,

> *'Tremendous amendments are required now from all of you. Uniting and being one. Loving one another, believing in Me, believing in My Heavenly Works, for I am among you always.'*

On September 11, 1991, the same day as the warning regarding the Twin Towers, Jesus also gave me a second warning about the tsunami.

> *'The islands, the sea and the continents will be visited by Me unexpectedly with thunder and by flame. Listen closely to My last words of warning, listen now that there is still time. Read our Messages and stop being scornful or deaf when Heaven speaks ... Soon, very soon now, the Heavens will open and I shall make you see The Judge.'*

Then on December 24, 1991, the eve of Christ's birth, I received a third warning. It was significant that it was given on Christmas Eve. I came to understand that Jesus was very unhappy about the way Christians have come to celebrate Christmas these days. While they should be going to church and worshiping His Holy Name, many treat Christmas as a holiday of leisure and consumption, offending Christ by giving more importance to decorating Christmas trees, exchanging gifts, and eating until sick rather than praising Jesus and honoring His Birth.

Christ has said the Enemy is slowly but steadily working to abolish His Name. Starting some years back, Christmas cards began omitting the name of Christ. Today they read 'Season's Greetings' under the pretext 'not to offend other religions,' as if anyone is really offended when Christians practice what they believe and 'keep Christ in Christmas'. There are many such efforts to strip the Name of Jesus out of society, and these efforts are part of the devil's attempt to abolish Jesus' Name. People ask, 'Where is the Antichrist and when is he coming?' My answer is, 'He's already at work among us, working to abolish Christ in our world.' This is why Christ's warning of December 24, 1991 said the following:

> *'Today I come with peace-terms and a Message of Love, but the peace I am offering is blasphemed by the earth, and the Love I am giving them is mocked and jeered in this Eve of My Birth. Mankind is celebrating these days without My Holy Name. My Holy Name has been abolished and they take the day of My Birth as a great holiday of leisure, worshipping idols. Satan has entered into the hearts of My children, finding them weak and asleep. I have warned the world ...'*

The fourth and final warning, which referred to the tsunami and other future events, came on February 18, 1993:

> *'See the days are coming when I am going to come by thunder and fire but I will find, to My distress, many of you unaware and in deep sleep! I am sending you, Creation, messenger after messenger to break through your deafness, but I am weary now of your resistance and your apathy ... Intoxicated by your own voice you have opposed My Voice but it shall not be forever – soon you shall fall ... My Church is in ruin because of your division ...*
>
> *'The earth will shake and like a shooting star will reel from its place, extirpating mountains and islands out of their places. Entire nations will be annihilated; the sky will disappear like a scroll rolling up as you saw it in your vision daughter. A great agony will befall on all the citizens, and woe to the unbeliever! Hear Me: and should men say to you today: "ah,*

but the Living One will have Mercy upon us, your prophecy is not from God but from your own spirit", tell them: although you are reputed to be alive, you are dead; your incredulity condemns you, because you refused to believe in My time of Mercy and prohibited My Voice to spread through My mouthpieces to warn and save My creatures ...'

According to scientists, when the earthquake happened under the sea in the Indian Ocean, causing the tsunami, the whole earth shook, stopped for a split second and went out of its normal axis. The shifting of the earth's plates caused a rupture more than 600 miles long, displacing the seafloor above the rupture by perhaps 10 yards horizontally and several yards vertically. The island of Sumatra and other islands moved several meters from their original place. This was a catastrophic event, one that should certainly grab our attention.

The tsunami news shocked and dismayed us all, but no one can say that God does not send us warnings. He sends warnings by those He chooses as mouthpieces, but often our response is: 'We have no need of these warnings; we have the Holy Bible and the writings of the Church Fathers, we never lack in offering sacrifices and prayers so what has Christ to tell us more than He has already given us?' Not only do they shut their ears but they prohibit God's Word from going out, placing obstacles upon obstacles.

After the tsunami hit Sumatra and went all the way to Africa, the world watched apocalyptic scenes on television. The distress and horror of seeing this natural disaster victimizing both inhabitants and vacationers in the space of mere minutes, was deeply distressing – especially learning that many of the victims were children. Yet then we also witness the 'miracles' that follow: a twenty-day-old baby found alive, floating on a little mattress; a little Swedish boy found alive and well; people pulling together to selflessly help those in need. The tragedy reminds us of how frail and small we human beings are – totally dependent on God's plans – and the miracles raise our hearts to praise God and our fellow man.

But unfortunately, when a disaster of this magnitude hits, and claims innocent lives, some people immediately put the blame on God, rather than on sinful humanity. For many it will be the only time they ever remember God, speaking of Him in anger, thus offending Him even more. You hear them say, 'If God is good, how could He allow such things?' At the same time, pain and sorrow sometimes make people say things they do not mean.

These tragedies, as hard as they are, can be opportunities for grace. But if only we would heed God's warnings, some of them could be averted altogether.

In that same prophecy of February 18, 1993, God also spoke of an 'Hour of Darkness' that will come over the earth if we do not change our hearts and return to Him:

> *'The sixth seal is about to be broken and you will all be plunged into darkness and there will be no illumination, for the smoke poured up out of the Abyss will be like the smoke from a huge furnace so that the sun and the sky will be darkened by it; … I will crush you to the ground to remind you that you are not better than vipers … you will suffocate and stifle in your sins; … When the hour of Darkness comes, I will show you your insides; I will turn your soul inside out and when you will see your soul as black as coal, not only will you experience a distress like never before, but you will beat your breast with agony that your own darkness is far worse than the darkness surrounding you. I will make human life scarcer than ever before; then when My wrath will be appeased, I will set My Throne in each one of you and together with one voice and one heart and one language you will praise Me, the Lamb.'*

What I understand from this passage is that a Day of Warning will come to reveal to us in a special way our true selves and what we carry in our soul. The wicked will be tormented and shocked when the condition of their soul is revealed to them in the Light of God.

God continues to call out in the night of our soul, peering through the window of our heart, reminding us that we are not only endangering the earth, but the whole cosmos! On March 8, 2000, the Lord said:

'Heaven has never leaned down so close to the earth as it is leaning now. Some time ago I could hear from earth a sigh or two, but now, I hardly hear anything. This is why I am moved to pity you, generation. What I hear from the corpse in a bragging tone is: "Look! I can live in a desert like the pelican; I can live in a ruin like the screech owl; I can live without God for I can do better than God."'

On February 7, 2002, God gave the following warning for the world and the USA:

'Your nation governs in complete opposition to all My Law of Love which differs from your outlandish system of laws; laws that commit the most heinous crimes to the point of endangering not only the earth but the stability as well of the whole cosmos; … I see from above how your designs will turn against yourselves; the world already is tasting the fruits of its own course, provoking nature to rebel with convulsions, drawing upon yourselves natural catastrophes, choking itself with your own scheming. I had beckoned you for years now but very few took notice; this purification that is now like a scourge upon you, generation, will draw many towards Me and those who spurned My warnings will return to Me in their distress …'

The whole world is now decaying in its evil. Ironically, the world is calling for peace, yet our sins keep us from achieving it. On September 30, 2002, the Lord told me:

'… those who stand up on platforms proclaiming peace … when these very ones are transgressing My commandments and are at war with Me; how do they expect in their right mind to bring peace?'

When Jesus approached me back in the eighties, He was warning us, even then, that the Father's Cup was already becoming full. Many times He said that we are provoking His Justice, which will draw upon us the Chastisement of Fire. At that time, however, it was conditional. Then, after fifteen years had passed, Jesus said that God's Justice couldn't be withdrawn altogether because His Message had not been heeded.

The Chastisement can, however, be diminished. How? By amending our lives, by repenting and living a True Life in God. We can diminish the Fire by acts of reparation, acts of genuine love, prayer, and especially through the reconciliation of the Churches uniting around one Altar.

On January 7, 2008, the Virgin Mary woke me up just after 3.10 am. She told me that we are very near the events that have been foretold that are facing humanity and that they are outside our door; events that are drawn by the world's rejection of God's Word, the world's spite, hypocrisy and godlessness. She said that '*The earth is in danger and will suffer from fire.*' She also said that '*God's wrath cannot be sustained any longer and that it will fall on us because man refuses to break with sin*' and that '*God's Mercy all of these years was to draw as many as possible to Him, extending His Arm to save them, but only a few listened.*'

> '*His time of Mercy will not hold much longer and the time is coming when everybody will be tested and the earth will spew out from within rivers of fire and the people of the world will understand their worthlessness and their helplessness for having lived without God in their hearts. God is firm and true to His Word. The time has come where the household of God will be tested and those who refused His Mercy will taste God's Fire.*'

At this point I asked about the people of the Church who persecute us and are blind to His Works of Mercy. Our Lady answered that '*they too will undergo what they deserve*'. Our Lady continued to speak about sacrifice. She has asked me to '*remind everyone that God our Creator asks us to commit ourselves more fully to Him, and that to be converted is not enough without sacrifice and steady prayers. There are various ways of showing God their love and generosity;*' that '*those who truly love God are blessed and should not fear in those days.*' Our Blessed Mother said that '*those who persevere through hardships are blessed.*'

She is '*pleased with all the priests who share and promote the Works of God*'. They should '*remain confident because they have received special graces from the Spirit of God and that through the Spirit they grew stronger in the Lord and in His plan of salvation*'. Our Lady said that '*Christ grants them His peace. If anyone serves and immolates himself as an offering, the judgment that is to come by fire will not be so severe upon them for in their spirit they will be enjoying the call of God that brought them to life.*' Our Lady said that '*many have fallen away but many will be raised. Many have failed to keep the Word of God secure in their hearts and transgressed the Word given to them.*' That is what our Lady gave as Message.

On November 28, 2009 the Lord called me and gave me a prayer that I had to distribute, asking us to pray it and ask for His Mercy. This is what our Lord said:

> '*Address Me Vassula in this way:*
>
> *"Tender Father, lash not Your wrath on this generation, lest they perish altogether; lash not on Your flock distress and anguish, for the waters will run dry and nature will wither; all will succumb at Your wrath leaving no trace behind them; the heat of Your Breath will put aflame the earth turning it into a waste!* ***From the horizon a star will be seen; the night will be ravaged and ashes will fall as snow in winter, covering Your people like ghosts****; take Mercy on us, God, and do not assess us harshly; remember the hearts that rejoice in You and You in them! Remember Your faithful and let not Your Hand fall on us with force, but, rather in Your Mercy lift us and place Your precepts in every heart. Amen".'*

When I received this prayer, I knew in my heart that it was urgent. The sentence: '*from the horizon a star will be seen, the night will be ravaged and ashes will fall as snow in winter, covering your people like ghosts …*' struck me in particular while I was hearing it, because Jesus changed tone and became very grave. To me it seemed out of context from the rest of the prayer. So with the help of others we sent this prayer around the world and all prayer groups prayed it continuously.

Four months later, on March 20, 2010, the Eyjafjallajökull volcano in Iceland erupted and produced an enormous ash cloud. The region around that volcano was evacuated. Some people took videos nearby and one could not see properly a few meters ahead as clouds of ashes were in the atmosphere covering the people like ghosts. Everything was grayish and covered with ash. Air transportation was halted and the many plane cancellations caused losses of tens of millions of dollars. Travelers were stranded all over the world. Fruits, fish and other products began to rot in their warehouses. On April 14, 2010, as the volcano continued to erupt, a bright star was seen on the horizon in the Midwest of the USA. I believe this spectacular star was a warning, as the volcano continued to spit its ashes for one and a half years. But I believe our prayers were heard because a nearby bigger volcano did not erupt as expected.

In giving us this prayer, God knew that this meteorite was heading to earth. One should ask, 'Why has God given us this prayer to pray four months before, was it not so as to spare us from a huge disaster?' Many people in this world are living in apathy and in a spirit of lethargy. Many of the ecclesiastics are prohibiting God from speaking to His people and wrongly advise their people not to listen, preventing them in this way to know the Will of God.

However, worse will befall on this earth if we, like Pharaoh who in his stubbornness refused to listen to Moses, ignore the Signs of the Times; and it will be too late.

Despite the severity of these Messages, they are not meant to be prophecies of doom and gloom. God's sweetness and tenderness is manifest. These Messages and prophecies for our times are a gift from God who gives them to us in these difficult times. They all come out of His boundless Mercy to wake us up; they are a call that comes from His sublime Love. This is the Hour of Mercy, but it will be followed by the time of Justice, because God will not allow us to offend Him forever.

No one will be able to hinder God's plans. It is only a question of time. Jesus asks us, '*Generation, unity will come but in which way, by peace terms or by fire?*' It is up to us to choose. Do we want to change? If we do, *we need not fear.* We are God's and God is ours. The soul that yields to God will triumph.

15

Miracles

To further draw our attention, God has also granted many miracles and wonders surrounding my Mission; these have been performed by the Holy Spirit during my witnessing, or through prayers. The following are some examples of these miracles.

I was invited to speak in America, in a little chapel in Independence, Missouri, on January 11, 1992. At the end of my talk, a pretty young woman came over to me holding a four-year-old boy, who was her son, wrapped in a blanket. His name was Curt. That day, as on other days, he had fever and was unable to walk or even wear shoes. He was in great pain. She was devastated and her face was swollen with tears. Accompanying her was a little nun, Sr. Mary Lucille, who spoke on her behalf.

'The boy is dying; he has crippling juvenile rheumatoid arthritis.'

He had been diagnosed at Children's Mercy Hospital in Kansas City, Missouri, at the age of two.

I was shocked because the boy must have understood, for he turned his face towards me and looked at me. Sr. Lucille continued,

'Will you please pray over him and give the boy a blessing on his forehead?'

The mother was not in control, as she was weeping so hard. I sighed with compassion, and then I stretched out my hand to make the sign of the Cross on his forehead, pleading desperately within me to the Lord and to our Blessed Mother: 'Do something!' I said. Just those two words. The boy was instantly cured, but we did not know it.

Curt and his mother left the chapel to go home, but once there Curt did not lie down as he usually did; instead he stood up and spoke, asking his mother for food and drink. The bewildered mother grabbed her child and rushed to the hospital to have him checked. His blood tests showed no trace of the disease anymore.

Now, I know what I did and said, but what they saw and heard me say was another story. This is what they witnessed: they saw me, after having blessed Curt on the forehead, taking Curt's hands one after the other, and making the sign of the Cross on his palms. Apparently I then lifted the blanket and made the sign of the Cross on the soles of his feet. Having done that I seemed to have lifted the blanket again and made a big sign of the Cross on his backbone. Then I turned to the mother and using the word 'when' not 'if', I said to her, 'When your boy becomes well, teach him the Rosary.' I had no idea that most of this had taken place. But the little boy was cured and later told his mother, 'Mom, when I looked at the Lady, She was very beautiful. When She touched my back, Her hands were cold and it hurt.' (He probably felt some pain during the healing.) 'Then this beautiful Lady asked me if I wanted to have a glimpse of Heaven and She took me up and I saw Angels.' I staggered when I heard their version of what happened, two months later.

This was a miracle that God performed completely in silence. The mother and the nun, together with the boy, went to many cities in the USA witnessing to the miracle. The complete hospital file was given to me and I gave it to the Vatican, but I never received a reply from them acknowledging receipt of the file. I kept a copy of that file, however. I met the boy several times afterward and the last time I saw him he was taller than me and a wonderful, good-looking teenager. We had a soft drink together and he asked me, 'What does God want from me, since He healed me?' I laughed and said to him, 'Just love Him and be happy. He has given you your life back. It is His gift, so be happy.'

Curt's grandfather wrote the following version of the miraculous healing for an American magazine:

'On this day, January 11, 1992, Sr. Lucille took my daughter by the hand, as she carried my grandson to Vassula, who asked, "What is the problem?" Vassula then prayed to God the Father, Jesus, and the Blessed Mother for healing. Through her prayers, Curt was healed. He is off the medication and all health problems related to the arthritis have vanished. Through Vassula's prayers, Curt has been given a gift from God. It is only one example of God's total Love and Mercy.'

Curt has seen our Blessed Mother, and has also received the gift of being able to see other people's Angels as well as his own.

So many miraculous healings have taken place during the years of my witnessing, but only Curt's parents went to the trouble of obtaining the hospital file and giving it to me. All others who were healed went away feeling happy, but never thought to obtain medical files and give them to me.

Another story concerns a Lebanese woman who lived in Stockholm, Sweden. She had water in her lungs. Her daughter had read the Messages and when I was invited to speak in a church in Stockholm, she did not want to miss my talk. She was dressed and ready to go when her sick mother asked her to stay at home to keep her company. The daughter, however, had made up her mind to go hear my talk and there was no way of convincing her otherwise. The mother refused to stay alone and decided to accompany her daughter, who felt rather annoyed, knowing that her mother's poor condition would delay them.

When they arrived, the church was packed. Unable to find two seats together, they were obliged to sit apart from each other. It is interesting to note that the mother did not know anything about me – about 'Vassula', or indeed whether my name indicated a man or a woman. She later told her daughter that when she looked at me speaking it was a Man with a beard she saw in my place. As she looked at Him she felt something happening in her lungs. She felt better and better during my talk and was spontaneously healed. When my talk was over, she rushed to her daughter, dancing, and trying to tell her that she was healed. Her daughter could not believe how her mother, from one minute to the next, had received her health back and had become full of life and vigor. When the mother said that she had seen a Man with a beard, they understood it was Jesus. I only heard the story the following morning, before leaving Stockholm. The daughter joyfully told me about the miracle.

From there I traveled to Copenhagen, Denmark, where my meeting took place in the afternoon. Before I began my witnessing of the Messages, I told the gathering about the miracle in Stockholm. Among those present was an elderly lady who had cancer on her palate. She was due to go to hospital early next morning for an operation. When she heard the story of the miracle, her heart was moved and she simply mumbled to herself, 'I wish something like this would happen to me too.' The next morning her friend dropped in to take her to the hospital, but amazingly the woman could no longer see any sign of cancer in her mouth and when she spoke to her friend it did not cause any pain. Her friend also noticed that her speech was better; she now articulated properly. When she finally did go to the hospital, the doctor checked her mouth and was amazed that he could no longer see any trace of the cancer on her palate.

Around the world while witnessing, our Lord has given many other cures: A retired doctor in the USA with leukemia was cured, just with a blessing and a prayer over him; in Chicago, a deaf boy, around fourteen years old, was cured when I laid my hands on him and prayed; at a Pittsburg conference I prayed over a man who had attended on crutches, and when he went to bed that night the pain in his legs disappeared and he was healed.

Unfortunately I didn't receive any of their hospital files, which reminds me of the time when Jesus cured the ten lepers. There were nine Jews and one Samaritan, and having been cured by Jesus they all left without thanking Him – with the exception of the Samaritan, who came back to thank Jesus. I heard the Lord say: '*Grace is offered to everyone ...*'

16

The Narrow Path

When you work for peace, you will be persecuted. I am not a bigot, but I was accused of being one. I am not a liar, yet I was accused of pretending to hear God's voice. I still have my wits about me – if I may say so – yet I was treated as a lunatic. I have no intention of undermining the Orthodox Church to which I belong, yet an Orthodox monk accused me of being a Trojan Horse paid by the Pope to lure the poor Orthodox into becoming Roman Catholics. People have written articles asking for my Church to excommunicate me – some have even spread false rumors that I've already been excommunicated. I've even received death threats – in three different countries!

The Lord reminds us that the path that leads to Eternal Life is narrow, filled with trials. One day, I really felt tired and worn out from all the trials that seemed to accumulate on me, so knowing that Jesus holds infinite power in His Hands and that He is able to sort out things and smoothen up my way, and like so many people, I went and complained to Him. He replied:[1]

> *'Grace does not go without suffering; oh, what will I not do to My closest ones, to My dearest friends!'*

I then said: 'Then, allow me to take the words of Saint Teresa of Avila and tell You, "No wonder You have so few friends!"' Jesus undisturbed replied:

1 September 25, 1992

'All men are weak ... Nevertheless, I will reply to your comment and tell you: if your soul only knew what I am offering and doing to you, you would have been the one to ask Me for more trials, sufferings, crosses, the lot! – I discipline those I love so do not object to what seems good to Me.'

And another time He added:

'I, the Lord, am showing you the steps I have taken for My Passion. Since you are serving Me, you must follow Me. What do you want Me to say: "follow Me but not in My Footprints?" This cannot be – whosoever serves Me, will follow My Blood-stained Footsteps."[2]

Out of our sacrifices and trials, the Lord derives great achievements for ourselves, for the others, and the Church. The Messages have thus continued to spread throughout the world, obtaining their victory. Many souls have been transformed into new Apostles to join the race in this spiritual battle. These Apostles have derived immense blessings and extraordinary favors from God; they have become part of a divine plan to reach everyone, even for the worst sinners, with peace, love, and sanctity so that the Church may be revived and have the power to overcome the evil that attacks it.

The Lord commanded,[3]

'Serve My House so that it recovers its vigour by reminding It that My Presence lights up any darkness ...'

'Serve My House and speak in My Name so that I, in My transcendent Love may continue to pour My blessings on this generation.'

We must learn that sacrificial love counts in God's eyes, fidelity to the Spirit of God requires giving up our own will, dying to ourselves, and putting God first in our life. God is a plus in our lives not a minus. I have had to learn this lesson myself. I've had to follow God's orders,

2 June 3, 1993

3 October 20, 1998

trusting Him, and trusting that He would provide all the necessary resources of His Wisdom, His support, and the tenderness of His love.

Unity is my mission, but to accomplish God's Will the largest of the Churches – the Roman Catholic Church – would have to play a central role. The sudden appearance of a revelation coming from God usually unsettles people. My work has been on the Vatican's radar for many years. They have issued a Notification calling the Messages into question, but I had yet to communicate directly with them. They had not consulted with me, nor had they deeply studied my case, as their Canon Law indicates what should be done in situations like mine.

Christ Himself had given His disciples guidance for how to discern a true prophet from a false one. He said that a true prophet, like a good tree, will bear good fruit, meaning that the person's messages and mission will have a positive effect in people's spiritual lives, bringing them closer to God. It takes years or even decades to see what the long-term fruit of a person's mission will be, but eventually it becomes clear whether the mission is bringing good fruit or bad. This is why the Church often conducts years of investigation before passing judgment on mystical happenings such as mine.

'Time is racing by and we are running out of time,' I told one of my priest friends, 'and if the world does not wake up from its lethargy and repent, all the evil coming from the earth will sooner or later fall upon us! So very few listen. The Lord wants His Mystical Body united. He keeps saying to His Shepherds that He does not want them to be as administrators running His Church, but as shepherds who care for their flock, but they do not listen! And now this Notification … The earth is challenging God's Justice and provoking Him, even nature is rebelling against us.' I picked up to read out to him part of a Message that God gave on April 15, 1996; the Lord said:

'I have kept silent and have shut My Eyes so far, I have drawn back many times My Hand from falling upon you, generation, and so many times I have receded My decisions to redress

> *you by fire; … Soon My Voice will be heard saying: "Enough! Enough is enough!" The earth will be rent and those who rebelled against Me will see My Hand falling on them; but the vessels of My Son I will uphold; I will come in a tempest of Fire; for some, this will come as a blessing, but for those who never feared Me, that Day, they will learn to fear Me …'*

The priest sighed, and then said, 'Are you surprised? History is being repeated. How many times in history have policies of prudence been ignored and Canon Laws broken? The rigidity of any organization acting in this way does not reveal its strength, but its frailty. Then the character of His prophet lies in the capacity to be as inflexible as a Church, but alone against all, to witness that only God gives the prophet the strength to resist men.'

Yet, in spite of growing obstacles, Christ's Voice would be constantly encouraging me not to fear but to continue spreading His Word to a dying world. When I felt that nothing was moving and showed my impatience He tried to reason with me and said,

> *'I am sending you precisely for this reason; I am sending you to the nations to declare that My Word is alive! So stand your ground and do not waver or fear, I am your Shield … your race is not over.'*[4]

Then on August 12, 1998, while I was in Rhodes, Jesus surprised me and said:

> *'I am sending you in a country*[5] *where you would stretch your shoots beyond the sea; … I will send you to them so that the olive tree once more produces its olive and the vine its fruit … My Vassula, I tell you: at the favourable time I will send you to them, and you will show yourself.'*

I knew Jesus was talking about Rome, but I had no idea how I would get there, and *'show myself to them'*, as Jesus had said a few weeks before. Amazingly, not long after this Message, my husband told me

4 April 16, 1993

5 Italy.

he was offered a new job. 'Where?' I asked. 'Rome', he replied, 'with a contract for six years'. Once again, the Lord was arranging things. All I needed to do was cooperate with His plan!

Before making the move to Rome, while still living in Switzerland, I received a phone call from a Swiss priest by the name of Fr. Damian. He told me that he had read a book defending me and that after reading it he felt in his heart that he should do something to help me. He asked what he could do and I suggested he could pray for me. He asked me if I had ever met Cardinal Cassidy who was the head of the Pontifical Office of Christian Unity at the Vatican. 'No I haven't', I replied, 'I think he's not in favor of my work.' 'Well,' said the priest, 'he must have been misinformed about you. He's a good friend of mine. Would you like to meet him if I arrange an appointment?' 'Well yes, of course, if he is willing to meet me.'

Soon after, Fr. Damian went to Rome, and when he returned he told me that Cardinal Cassidy preferred that I first meet with Msgr Fortino who worked in his office, and he gave me his phone number.

As it was summer time, I was just leaving for a holiday in Rhodes. Upon my arrival there, I dug into my purse and felt something odd. As I pulled out my hand, I saw that it was covered with a thin, red laterite sort of sand. I looked in my purse and to my great amazement I saw a mass of cocoons made of this same red substance, some of them broken, and hundreds of small, black dead spiders scattered throughout, with the exception of one, which was much bigger, probably the mother. I knew right away that this was a satanic manifestation. My purse had never left my hand from the moment I left Switzerland until I arrived in Rhodes, and I was certain that no hand could have put the cocoons in my handbag. I suspected witchcraft – black magic – because it had simply manifested itself out of nowhere. This was later confirmed by a renowned exorcist, who said that he believed it was an evil manifestation done by someone who worked with Satan and against me. My friends who witnessed this were quite shaken. I prayed over the purse, rebuking the devil through the power of Jesus, and then emptied out the cocoons, dust and all the spiders into the trash bin. I never used that handbag again and a month later I saw that this black, leather handbag had turned greenish and looked worn out. I could tell that Satan was very displeased that the Vatican doors were opening to me, and that whatever misunderstandings were still hanging as a thick black cloud in there at the Vatican, could soon be clarified.

The next day I called the Vatican to speak to Msgr Fortino in Rome. I was wondering how our conversation would turn out. Msgr Fortino himself picked up the phone, and after introducing myself I said that I had been asked to phone him. To my surprise, although he was Bulgarian, he spoke to me in Greek. He was very friendly. We set a date to meet when I would be in Rome. It seemed as if Christ was making my narrow path easy, I thought.

God has His time and His agenda. Within a week after moving to Rome, I found myself parked just outside Msgr Fortino's office at the Vatican. His office was in a very old building, typical of the Vatican architecture, and stood just a few meters from the great basilica of St Peter's. I approached the doorman and gave him the details of my appointment. He ushered me to an old-fashioned, wooden elevator that creaked its way up to the second floor where I rang the bell at the Unity Office suite. Another doorman answered the bell and invited me to wait in a small sitting room. Almost immediately Msgr Fortino came, greeting me with a very warm smile. He was short and stout. He asked me to follow him, and as we walked he gave me a short history of every icon we passed on our way to the official meeting hall. Finally we entered the hall and sat at a huge, oblong table used for official Vatican business.

Msgr Fortino was known to be a very humble and good man, *reachable and friendly*. He was the type of person who immediately makes you feel at ease. His first words, spoken with humor were, 'Your name has made a lot of noise here in the Vatican.' I replied, 'Oh good, finally ...' I might have sounded impertinent, but I couldn't resist feeling happy because this is where the Lord had wanted me to be, and somehow through His grace it had come to pass. I could now tell those in the Vatican the truth and clarify what the Messages are all about and tell them what the Lord was asking. This was the fulfillment of Jesus' words to me that I would be sent to the Eternal City and He would guide me to those who were questioning my mission.

We had an interesting dialogue and I could see that Msgr Fortino was open to the Messages. To my surprise, he had even read some of them. Our conversation was very friendly, and just before I left he said, 'Vassula, the doors of this Office will always remain open for you. You may come in anytime you wish and talk to me; I want to make your life easier.' I felt that he was fully aware of all the persecutions that were coming against me.

With this invitation, I used to drop in the Unity Office quite often, informing Msgr Fortino of the latest happenings of my mission. One day, he finally arranged a meeting with Cardinal Cassidy, the 'boss' of that Office.

The day I went to meet him I rang the bell at the Unity Office, and Msgr Fortino came out to greet me. Apologetically he said, 'I am so sorry, but Cardinal Cassidy had an appointment with his doctor, but come in, he will be back soon.' He led me to a small sitting room. After half an hour the door opened and in came Cardinal Cassidy. I greeted him, and noticed that he avoided looking at me eye to eye. I started to introduce myself more thoroughly but he abruptly stopped me and said, 'Just come to the facts, I have no time.' I replied, 'I wanted to see you because I am dealing with *your* people,' meaning Catholics. I said these words to make him look at me, and he did. I continued, 'I'm glad to tell you all about my calling,' and I told him about my mission. I emphasized the ecumenical pilgrimages, and how all the clergy from different Church denominations were asking forgiveness from one another and how they were gathering together to pray around one Altar.

Suddenly, he turned angry and said, 'With these sorts of performances you are harming our progress in unity!' I was shocked. Raising my voice, I said, 'What is your aim for unity? Isn't it to be reconciled and sharing around one Altar?' 'Yes! But not yet, not just like that!' he replied. But I insisted, 'Unity is easy when there is love'. He got up and said, 'I must go now.' I remained calm and said, 'Next time you have a dialogue of unity in your office, I would like to be there too.' This was of course far-fetched and I knew it. He replied, 'Deal with Msgr Fortino, he is a good advocate for you,' and then left the room.

I went home and wrote him a letter in which I added a paragraph from the Messages quoting Christ's request for unity in the Church. I told the Cardinal that I was very disappointed with the way he received me. In the meantime, Msgr Fortino was dying to know what happened and he called me. When I recounted the meeting, he was quite disappointed and said, 'It is obvious he has been influenced by the negative reports. Don't worry, I will talk to him.' A week later Msgr Fortino called me back and said, 'Vassula, everything is clear now. Cardinal Cassidy is waiting to see you any time.'

A short time later, a Greek Orthodox Archimandrite was visiting me in Rome and wanted to meet Cardinal Cassidy. I called the Unity Office and arranged to drive him there. When I saw the Cardinal this time, he was completely loveable – I can't think of a better word. He seemed to have a new opinion of me this time. He invited me to join them in the meeting, but I declined, saying this was not a meeting for me, and I went to wait in another room. Later they took a picture and I purposely stayed out of the picture so the Cardinal wouldn't think I wanted to use a picture with him to promote myself. As we left, we were all in good spirits.

I was happy to have this new rapport with Cardinal Cassidy. My thoughts went back to those days in Bangladesh when my Angel first called me, and I reflected on how things had developed since then. It was a difficult, narrow path, but I did not fear, for near me, holding my hand, was Jesus. Going along that narrow path the Lord had achieved so many triumphs, so many conversions of people's hearts and souls. Now God had arranged for His Messages to reach the authorities of His Church in Rome, in the very office where the Church works for the Christian Unity which Christ Himself was asking for in the Messages. I was overjoyed!

But my joy did not last long. With each step of progress in my mission, new trials assailed me. No sooner were these Vatican connections being made than all kinds of personal problems started manifesting. My first cousin's son suddenly died while driving his motorbike on safari in the African desert. My mother lost her sight, was confined to a wheelchair and had to be placed in a nursing home. From that time on, I would travel once a month from Rome to Switzerland to spend time with her and bring her joy in her suffering. At the same time, my older sister and her husband both became very ill with cancer. The doctors had to operate on my sister and take away her stomach. She then underwent chemotherapy treatments and her health slowly melted away until four years later both she and her husband died within three days of each other. It was devastating to watch them suffer this way, and due to my mother's sickness, we never told her they had died as we knew it would cause her even more suffering.

During this same period, my oldest son, Jan, came down with a fever and just two days after his marriage was diagnosed with Hodgkin's disease. He too had to undergo chemotherapy. It was so painful that it caused him to cry like a baby and require calming pills. One day when he was really depressed, he called me in tears and said in desperation, 'I am your son! How is it that God allows this to happen to me when you are working so hard for Him?'

I was torn inside, but all I could do was continue trusting in God. So day by day I prayed for Jan and wondered what would happen next. Would the Lord take him from me? Would I be asked to accept that cross? The Lord had not revealed the answer to me, until finally one day while I was on the phone with Jan I heard the most wonderful words a mother could ever hear. The good Lord whispered to me and said, '*Your son will be all right again.*' I was elated and felt like Mary must have felt when She knew that Her Son Jesus would rise again. The Lord kept His word, and my son recovered.

But just a few months later, my younger sister Helen, who lived in Switzerland, called me and said, 'Mother's not eating or drinking; she may be dying.' I left Rome for Switzerland at once. When I arrived, my mother was emaciated and her eyes were closed. I spoke to her, but she did not recognize me and did not answer. She had completely disconnected from my sister and me. After some days with her, I had to leave for India for a mission trip that had been planned months before. When the time came to leave my mother's room it was the most painful and saddest moment of my life. With a heavy heart I looked at her, and not knowing if I'd see her again, I slowly walked out into the corridor. My heart was so heavy that no tears welled up, but my whole body was aching. I could not think or see in front of me anymore. I tried hard to focus on the fact that she would soon be with the Lord, but all I could feel was the pain of being separated from the one who had brought me into this world, the one who had raised me, protected me, and prayed for me through my whole life. As I flew on the plane back to Rome and then to India, I reflected on how much my life had changed from those days of my carefree youth. The Lord had given me so much, but the 'narrow path' to Heaven required great sacrifices as well. Four days later, my sister called me in India to say our mother had passed away.

Then, just a year after my mother's death, my brother suddenly died. I began to wonder if anyone in my family would remain alive. The Greek Orthodox priest who presided at my brother's funeral voiced the same concern as he mumbled, 'Enough is enough! When will all this stop?'

I connected all these mishaps to the witchcraft of the cocoons and the dead spiders. These satanists who aimed at my family and at me were using Satan's powers, and had almost taken my eldest son away. Our Lord, however, did not allow the devil to go that far.

It was extremely difficult to lose my brother, my mother, my sister, my brother-in-law, and my cousin, and to watch my own son almost die. Yet all I could do was to pray and trust in God. I could not turn my back on God or on the mission He had given me. I had to believe He was in control and He knew what was best for all of us. This is the choice we all have when we face our crosses in life. We can reject them, and curse God, or we can accept them and praise God. Our response can't change the crosses. I have learned about the value of the Cross from Jesus' own words. Sometimes He gives us His Cross to sanctify us and to lead us into prayer, and to bring us to a closer union with Him. Whatever our cross may be, God's reasons are always good.

Along with all these family trials, the trials coming from outside increased as well. Those who were opposed to my mission were enraged that I now had access to the Unity Office at the Vatican and could go there any time. So they increased their slander and attacks against me, even contacting the Vatican to persuade them to turn against me. This caused me a great deal of distress. I couldn't understand why people, who say that they work for unity, would oppose those who actually gather the Churches together, pray and work for a unity in diversity. 'Why do they carry this malice in their heart? Can't they see God's

Hand at work?' I asked my husband. 'What more will these people say?' Again I remembered the words of the Father when He said that they would hound me like game, rating me at a high reward for the one who will destroy me.

The Lord reminds us all, though: '*The proof that anyone is joined and one with Me, formed in Me and knit in Me is when your heart is grafted as well on My Cross with all its bearings; anyone who is convinced that He belongs to Me must understand that he belongs to My Cross as well …*'[6]

Despite the voices reaching the Vatican with opposition toward me, Cardinal Joseph Ratzinger, who was the Vatican's Prefect of the Congregation for the Doctrine of Faith (and would later become Pope Benedict XVI in the year 2005) decided to open a dialogue with me. He asked that I write my answers to five questions in order to get clarification on the issues which had been raised in the Vatican's original Notification, that had announced concerns about my work. My hope was that by providing these answers, the Vatican might modify their Notification or nullify it altogether.

After answering the Cardinal's five questions, I was told that he was pleased. When asked about the investigation, I was informed that his answer was, '*Tutto e positivo*' meaning all is positive.

With this good news I asked for a private audience with Cardinal Ratzinger, who had once said that he would only meet me when the questions raised in the Notification were satisfactorily answered. As this had now been achieved, I was granted a meeting with him in the year 2004. When I arrived he led me to a very distinguished sitting room and said to me in French, '*Finalement*!', meaning, 'Finally!' This meant a lot to me, and I praised the Lord, thinking, 'All that is happening shows the power and the authority of Jesus Christ.'

I would never have imagined that one day God would guide me into the heart of the Vatican, and that I would be speaking with the future Pope about matters concerning the Church. As Cardinal Ratzinger and I spoke, his simplicity and humility impressed me. Twice during the course of our meeting he said, 'The Church sometimes makes

6 November 11, 1998

mistakes but we ask God to forgive us.' I offered him the book *True Life in God* which contained the Messages in it and showed him that the new edition of the book now included my answers to the five questions, which he had requested I do. He said: 'Good, everybody should read this dialogue to find the truth in its light.'

As a result of this meeting with Cardinal Ratzinger, many of my detractors were silenced and eclipsed for a while. None of them admitted their mistake, though, nor did they rejoice at this positive result. On the contrary, they were heard saying, 'This is the apostasy', meaning that the Vatican had apostatized! Before, the same people used to trumpet out loud, 'Rome has spoken!' and everybody trembled, taking it in the same way as if they were told God has spoken. Now that it does not suit them, they say, 'Rome has apostatized.' However, many thousands of people worldwide who believed in the Messages, including many priests, were celebrating Rome's discernment and change in attitude.

In just two weeks' time, the period of my husband's work in Rome was coming to an end, and it would be time for us to leave.

Before my departure, however, Msgr Fortino made an appointment for me with Cardinal Kasper, who had replaced his old boss, Cardinal Cassidy. I found him to be a very cheerful man. I had no doubt the meeting had been arranged by our Lord to pass on His request: that the Churches work together to unify the date of Easter. For over 1,000 years, Easter has been celebrated on a different date by the Orthodox Church and the Roman Catholic Church (though occasionally those dates overlap). Jesus had told me many times that this discrepancy was symptomatic of the Church's disunity and was greatly weakening the Church's power in the world. I explained this Message to Cardinal Kasper. I told him that Jesus promised that if the Churches would establish one date for Easter, the Lord would do the rest. He would restore the unity between the Churches in a way that we could never do on our own and this would bring peace to the *whole* world.

'The Lord wants you to bring the Catholic Church to join the Orthodox Church and celebrate Easter together,' I told the Cardinal. Since his Office was responsible for building unity between the Churches, he was the perfect person to hear this Message. He stood up, and admiring an icon of the Resurrected Christ that I had brought him, smiled and said, 'But you have the wrong date!' I stared at him, and on behalf of my Greek Orthodox Church I said, 'But so do you!' He remained silent and I went on to say: 'Look, your Eminence, even so, the date does not matter as much as our celebrating this Feast together as we should. This is what Christ wants us to do, and if we do that, the Lord has promised that He will do the rest and unite us completely!' He reflected a moment before saying, 'I will bring what you suggested to the Holy Father, Pope John Paul II.' I got up, thanked him and left.

The Lord was triumphant. He had opened the door to deliver the Messages to the right people, and, in 2005, just a short time after my meetings with Cardinal Ratzinger and Cardinal Kasper, Pope John Paul II passed away, and Cardinal Ratzinger was elected Pope.

It seemed as if everything was moving in the right direction, but more trials remained ahead. Once Cardinal Ratzinger became Pope Benedict XVI, Cardinal William Levada became the Prefect for the Council for the Doctrine of the Faith (CDF). Despite the answers I had offered to the five questions, which were now printed in my book, Cardinal Levada decided to send out a letter to all the Catholic Bishops of the world in 2007, reiterating the Vatican's Notification of 1995, which seemed to contradict the positive rapport I had built with the CDF. As of the writing of this book, the situation with the Catholic Church is still in flux, as it is with my own Greek Orthodox Church. In some areas, I am harshly rejected by the Church leaders, yet in many other areas I continue to be supported by Bishops, priests, theologians and nuns who read the Messages, write me letters, attend prayer meetings, and join our pilgrimages to build Unity between the Churches.

As for those who opposed my mission, I try not to lose the peace that Christ has given me. I know God was asking me to have a spirit of forgiveness, love and compassion toward them.

Not long ago, God gave me a dream. This was one of the most striking visions I have ever had. I found myself in a courtyard, sitting on a bench in front of the entrance to a huge, beautiful Cathedral. It seemed as though I was living there, but also as though I belonged there and guarding it, for I was holding a couple of keys to the Cathedral's front gate.

My spirit was in a state of such total mental peace and stillness that nothing mattered to me anymore. I was enjoying the serenity that surrounded me while God was resting in me and I in Him. All past sufferings or joys, all powerful events or turmoil that had taken place in my life seemed to be like nothing anymore, they seemed to have lost their mark on me. Shrouded by tranquillity of mind I felt invulnerable and free of the world. A feeling of equanimity had invested me, a feeling of not belonging to anyone or anything. I felt free from all people whether they were enemies or friends, free from polemics or threats, free from becoming exhilarated in joy or from becoming desolate in sadness, free from death; in short, nothing mattered to me anymore, nothing impressed me anymore for I was God's and God was mine.

While in this tranquil state, enwrapped in this spirit, I saw five Cardinals hurriedly approaching the Cathedral, one of whom I recognized as Cardinal Joseph Ratzinger (now Pope Bendict XVI). They reached the gate of the Cathedral and intended to go in. I watched as Cardinal Ratzinger tried to open the Cathedral gate with a key. It did not fit, so he tried other keys, one key after the other, but none of them seemed to fit. All five Cardinals looked perplexed. Without a sound I stood up and walked slowly over to them without looking at them, while at the same time I could feel their eyes on me. I knew that they were wondering what I was doing there. I placed one of the keys I had in the keyhole without difficulty and clicked open the gate for them.

From this vision I understood that the leaders of the Church are not listening to Christ's Message that can lead them to Unity. The restoration of mutual love and humility are missing; that is the *right key* that will enable them to see the truth in a totally different light and achieve Unity. And ah! How much does the Lord Jesus know of the differences between the Churches! Yet He wants them to change their way of approaching one another. Christ showed them that *all* of them should *bend* and use the key of *humility and love*, none other.

Jesus says:

> *'I have never ceased appointing prophets, setting them in the way of the Truth for My Salvific Plan; I bring them to fulfill their noble vows that had risen to their lips at our Divine enamored encounter … Today you will recognize them by the zeal they have for My House. My House that dresses them, a zeal that devours them … They will not hide their face from trouble but they will endure with peace all the trials and their hearts shall not be broken but sanctified; nor will they break their vow of fidelity of sharing My Cross.*
>
> *'So if you happen to notice their wounds and you ask them, "Who has made those wounds on you?" they will all tell you, "I have offered my back to atone for you. These wounds you see I have received with savagery in the House of my Master's friends … it is because I have been telling them the truth that they made me an enemy and treated me as such. But it does not matter and I give no attention to my wounds because what is important to me is to know about the Cross, the Instrument of our Redemption; the Cross of our Redeemer … Obedience to God comes before obedience to men, say the Scriptures and so I have obeyed and followed the Heavenly instructions given to me."'*[7]

Whenever those voices of opposition seemed to get the better of me, God has always sent voices of people to support me. After long mission trips around the world, I would often return home exhausted and depleted. At such times, the love of my family was just what I needed. I remember how my son, Fabian, would come to me and say, 'You look tired, mom. Are you okay?' 'Yes, I'm okay,' I would reply. Not convinced, he would say, 'Look, for three days I will take over the kitchen. I will cook and clean up. So what would you like to have today, chicken and potatoes in the oven or spaghetti Bolognese?' I would choose one of them and he would not allow me to enter the kitchen or even pick up my cup to take it to the kitchen. He was only thirteen, but he too was growing to become a small apostle. Already

---

7 April 28, 2000

he had shared what he knew of the Messages with his best friends, and being youngsters they were interested in asking me many questions, which I always enjoyed answering.

'Never become discouraged,' I have tried to remind myself and others, 'because at the end of the tunnel there *will be light*. Persevere, never lose hope, and never let go of our Redeemer's sleeve. Cling to Him!'

There is always an Easter that follows Good Friday for those who believe. Always. It is God's promise to us. And God keeps His promises.

> *'I have invited you to My Banquet and through you many others … My Pillar, supporting My Cross of Unity, radiate the light of the Knowledge of My Glory, radiate in this darkness, the light of My munificence and do not fear; I have poured anointed oil in your mouth so that you may speak for Me; be My chantress, always of good cheer; sing to this generation by traveling round the world, relying on My Grace … when you speak, My love, keep always to the point; yes, repeat all My sayings but in few words; set the jewels I have given you in each heart; let everyone know that My Conversations are sweetness itself; I am with you …'*[8]

Only through God can we create a world of peace. Jesus said to everyone:

> *'I will remind My children that My compassion does not go by unmoved, for I am Father to them. I will make their heart sing for Me and they will realize that outside My Sanctuary their table is empty. They will understand that outside My Sanctuary they will stifle with sorrow and burdens; outside My Arms they will face Destruction and Death.'*[9]

> *'Tell them that the Prince of Peace, this God surrounded by Cherubim, laid aside His Crown and royal vestments to patrol the world barefoot and wearing sackcloth to manifest*

8 August 29, 1998.

9 October 6, 1993.

His grief. As I have treated you kindly and allotted you a place in My Sacred Heart so will I treat the rest of My children … and I will complete their journey with them.'[10]

10 October 11, 1993.

17

End of Times

A Voice from the heights of Glory called out that the Treasures of Heaven were kept for this End of Times. The Voice asked me to write everything down. It proclaimed:

> *'I am advancing like the clouds above you, yet many of you say you do not see Me, generation. You rove to and fro through the riches of the world, but when it comes to see the spiritual Treasures that can be poured on you to vest you with Myself in majesty, you pay no attention.'*[11]

The Lord goes on to explain that one of the noblest and most inestimable Treasures is the Knowledge of God, since with this Treasure one obtains God's intimate friendship and God Himself.

Then on April 3, 1996 the same Voice tells us what He had foreseen:

> *'It had been said that at the End of Times Our Hearts*[12] *would raise Apostles and they would be called Apostles of the End of Times.*
>
> *'These would be instructed by the Queen of Heaven and by Myself to go forward in every nation to proclaim without fear the Word of God. Even when they would be drenched with blood by the enemy's vicious attacks, they shall not be broken. Their tongue will pierce the enemies of My Church,*

11 March 2001

12 The expression 'Our Hearts' represents the Heart of Jesus and that of His Mother

like a double-edged sword, by exposing their heresies. They would never stagger nor would they know fear because I would provide them with a spirit of courage. The destructive whip would not catch them; they would not leave one stone unturned.

'They would pursue the sinners, the lofty speakers, the great and the proud, the hypocrites, the traitors of My Church; they would pursue them with My Cross in one hand and the Rosary in the other; and we would stand by their side. They would shatter the heresies and build faithfulness and truth in their place. They would be the antidotes of the poison, because they would sprout like buds from the Royal Heart of Mary.'

This Message of hope is really appropriate and in full coordination with what is happening today in this End of Times. God is raising and forming 'apostles' in an extraordinary way during these past years, naming them 'Apostles of the End of Times'. They are being formed and inspired by God to act in accordance with His Will and to put aflame the whole world, leading it into compunction and renunciation of all its previous sins. Their passage will raise a spiritual renewal, since the Holy Spirit will be their Guide, their Comforter and their Companion.

The term 'End of Times' does not mean that the world will stop or come to an end. It is understood as a particular time in history and an expression only. Right now, we are living in the End of Times, in the middle of a spiritual battle, unseen by the eye, but felt all around us and even more in our soul. In this battle between good and evil, we must choose one or the other. The battle depends on us. We alone have the ability to choose, as we can trace the outline of our life, and decide what we stand for, good or evil. In the end, the final outcome of this battle will be determined by our choices.

The spiritual battle of this End of Times is so violent that God has to intervene in an absolute and ineffable manner through His Holy Spirit. It is a time during which God's Grace and Mercy flow out abundantly like never before in history, calling everyone to repentance before it's too late. At the same time the Holy Spirit is distributing gifts on all mankind, even to the least; not only for a renewal, but also to bring us to know the Will of God.

We've had many signs showing us that we are living in the days the Scriptures speak about when the Antichrist is in full action and seeking to control the world forever.

Here are some words Christ gave me on April 19, 1992:

> *'The world has exchanged My Divinity for a worthless imitation: a mortal man. It has given up Divine Truth for a Lie; but, it has been said*[13] *that at the End of Time, Satan will set to work and that there will be all kinds of miracles and a great deal of a deceptive show of signs and portents and everything evil that can deceive those who are bound for destruction because they would not grasp the Love of the Truth which could have saved them ...*
>
> *'The power of the Rebel [Antichrist] is such that he has, without any fear, appeared openly now to everyone, this is the one of which the prophet Ezekiel*[14] *spoke, the one swollen with pride, the one who claims to be God, the one who apes the Truth, the one who considers himself as My equal and says that he sits on My Throne. The Rebel is indeed the Enemy of My Church, the Antichrist, and the man who denies the Holy Trinity. Have you not read: the man who denies that Jesus is the Christ, he is a liar, he is the Antichrist and he is denying the Father as well as the Son because no one who has the Father can deny the Son, and to acknowledge the Son is to have the Father as well.'*

With this I would like to explain that the Scriptures might be referring to an evil movement, whose adepts are influenced by Satan himself, disregarding every single one of God's Commandments. Thus they would be waging war against God's people and turning the world into chaos. We only have to listen to the news, to see this modern deterioration of human values, and how evil wants to prevail.

---

13 2 Thessalonians 2: 9–12

14 Ezekiel 28

Science and technology create for us immeasurable material comfort. But often personal material comfort replaces the true interests of mankind's moral and spiritual knowledge. All human beings want to live peacefully, feeling happy and loved, but some want to obtain their happiness by using unethical methods which can be cruel, and abominable in God's Eyes. Some obtain their happiness at any cost; they would not hesitate to inflict suffering upon others in their quest to satisfy their selfish intentions.

Sometimes it seems that the world has been turned upside down. People say, 'So much injustice and so much sorrow ...' Yes, this is what I mean when I speak about the invisible, yet ever present spiritual battle that we are living in. Let me clarify the situation by quoting the Virgin Mary's own words given on May 15, 1990:

> *'The world has grown cold, icy cold ... the world is dead to love. It lies in deep obscurity because hatred, greed and selfishness dominate the entire earth all the way to its core. I am shaken by terrible sights with the iniquities of this dark world and the apostasy that penetrated in the sanctuary itself. The disasters, famines, afflictions, wars and plague, all these are drawn by you. The earth is autodestructing itself and it is not God who gives you all these disasters, as many of you tend to believe. God is Just and all Merciful but evil draws evil.'*

The devil is once more deceiving the world with the same lie with which he deceived Eve: that we can be God and in turn do not need God.

Imagine for a moment that all the people who do evil deeds did good deeds instead, every selfish person became unselfish, all acts of greed on earth became an act of charity and every act of injustice became an act of justice. Do you not agree with me that if this situation existed, there would be no more hungry and homeless people on earth? Can you imagine science being applied to give early warnings about natural disasters rather than to manufacture weapons and fight wars?

If people faced the reality of love in God and in men, they would be led to love God and one another. If people answered God's request for prayer and prayed, this world would be a 'paradise' and a hymn of thankfulness to God. If one accepted that there must be Unity between the Christian Churches, there would already be a hope of the fulfillment of Jesus' promise: 'one fold and one Shepherd'.[15] If people accepted God the way these Apostles of the End of Times recommend, God would already be 'everything in everyone.'[16] If people took God's warning about Satan seriously, the latter would already be banished from men's hearts and from the world. If people would heed God's calling to conversion, all men and women would already be Saints. If everyone shared in what God says today in His Messages, the personal history of each one of us, and consequently the history of all humankind would be a Song of Love.

On July 21, 1990 the Lord gave me a very frightening vision. I saw that I was looking outside a window. It was daylight, but suddenly the earth started to shake violently beneath my feet. The ground was going up and down and I heard a Voice saying that the earthquake was of a magnitude of 8 on the Richter scale. *It was not stopping.* Again I looked out the window at the sky and saw how it was losing its luminosity. I stared up at the heavens and saw they were becoming darker by the second, until they reached the depth of full night. Then as I watched the stars, I saw them falling, or rather they seemed to speed away from the eastern horizon to the western horizon. It was as though they were leaving the heavens. Then the tremors stopped and there was a menacing stillness in the darkness. I noticed that I had a very faint light in my room. I looked out of the window and saw there were just a few houses in the whole town showing a weak light.

Later, on August 4, 1990, these words were given to me:

> *'Justice is soon to descend – Ecclesia shall revive; the earth shall be set aflame.'*

And again, on December 13, 1992, the Lord is urging us:

15 John 10: 16

16 1 Corinthians 15: 28

'Generation, you have still not set your minds for Me – when will you decide to return to Me? Do you want to pass this era's threshold by blazing Fire, by brimstone and devouring flame?'

On June 3, 1993, I heard the Voice of God saying:

'Woe to the unrepentant – their corpses will litter this desert, this desert they themselves laid out. My Angel then will fill the censer he has been holding in front of My Throne and the altar – with Fire he will throw down on to the earth and while everybody will be watching, a violent earthquake will come, and the elements of the earth will catch fire and fall apart. Many will take to the mountains to hide in caves, and among the rocks – they would call out to Me but I will not listen.'

Many warnings such as this one have been given to us repeatedly, warning against self-destruction. Again the Voice on June 3, 1994 called out:

'I do not come to condemn the world, since I am here to save the world. I am here now to warn the world … stay awake praying at all times for the strength to survive all that is going to happen.'

And again I hear our Father in Heaven say sadly:

'I look at the earth today and wish I never did … My Eyes see what I never wanted to see and My Ears hear what I dreaded to ever hear! My Heart as a Father sinks with grief. I fashioned man to have My Image, yet they have degraded themselves and today so many of them have taken the likeness of the Beast!'[17]

In the Messages God has spoken about three distinct evil figures: the Antichrist, the Beast and the Dragon. Each one has his role to play in the End of Times. These three figures form a triangle.

17 April 15, 1996

Fr. José Antonio Fortea, a renowned exorcist, wrote in his book *Interview with an Exorcist,* that:

'The book of Revelation clearly distinguishes between the three key figures who will arise in opposition to Christ and the Church at the End of Time: the Antichrist, the Beast, and the Dragon (or Serpent). Whereas the Antichrist is a man, the Beast is a political power that brings war to the earth. It is the Dragon who is identified with the devil. There is no ambiguity or confusion in Revelation between these three distinct realities.'

It is difficult to interpret expressions, and the Bible uses many expressions, especially when they are referring to the devil. We have been entertained, now and then, by movies where the story presents the devil as procreating a son. This is impossible. We should not forget that the devil is a spirit and therefore remains one. As we have seen, however, he can enter human beings and possess them, or he can infest them, obsess them, or tempt them. Once possessed, the devil is in control and can easily act through them.

Saint Paul writes about the End of Times in 2 Thessalonians Chapter 2. He speaks about how we can distinguish when the End of Times are upon us, and says that there are two given Signs.

The first Sign is the great Apostasy (when people reject the Divine Truth), which we are in, and the second Sign is the spirit of rebellion where Satan will play God, imitating Him; even enthroning himself in God's seat and aping Him. The Lord taught me never to take a passage from the Scriptures out of context and try to understand or explain its full meaning. He also taught me to join it with other Bible passages, taken from here and there, so as to give a complete and full meaning.

In our present worldwide Apostasy and moral crisis the appeals for peace and the return to human values go unheeded, especially in the most industrially advanced countries. Holy Justice is provoked daily, hour after hour, adding sin upon sin. I sometimes wonder at God's patience and tolerance and am amazed how God tolerates us still and has not already wiped us all out by a major chastisement.

The Apostasy and spirit of rebellion are the major Signs of the End of Times that were mentioned in the book of Daniel. Cathedrals are sold, terrorism is expanding, natural disasters happen more often, and are becoming increasingly violent. Many of us are serving the non-existent gods of the philosophers. On June 1 2002, the Lord said,

> *'People in your days are in search of false gods, following all sorts of pagan systems, to obtain knowledge and power they think; then the world is ever so charmed by the beauty of crystals, the beauty of leaves, elements that they place above My Omnipotence, since they ask from these healing powers, instead of the gracious and healing power of My Holy Spirit; if they are impressed by their shape let them deduce from these how much mightier is He that has formed the crystals, the leaves and the like, the Author of them all! ...'*

Man tends to mount by means of ladders and climb up to possessions and treasures of this world that wear out and do not last instead of grasping the real treasures of Heaven.

The economic crisis is another big sign to humanity. The Almighty God is now shattering Mammon, who represents the god of money, and to whom the world has bowed low and worshipped, bringing egoism, wars and wickedness in the hearts, instead of the love of God.

However, in spite of the world's wickedness and godlessness, God still loves us and reassures us that He will rebuild what Satan tore down. This is what He said on May 6, 1992:

> *'Today Satan is vomiting all his hatred on the earth. He tears up and overthrows countries in his rage. He destroys and brings disaster after disaster, but with great power My Hand shall build up all that he has torn.'*

In the midst of our current Apostasy, our Lord gives us a Sign of hope in this End of Times: the Sign of hope is a renewal which the Lord calls 'Second Pentecost'. Unmerited gifts are being distributed to us such as: speaking in tongues, the gift of prophecy, the gift of healing, gifts of knowledge and so on. In short, what is given to us is all that is Celestial.

Even when a soul is spiritually dead and her 'stench of death' reaches heaven, now, in these times of grace and mercy, the Holy Spirit suddenly and unexpectedly descends on that soul and breathes a breath of resurrection within her to revive her. He then sets that soul aflame, burning to the root all that is evil and unholy. The Holy Spirit lifts her in His love and makes her taste God's sweetness. Transformed and flamed with the sweetness of God, that soul runs out with joy and becomes from thereon a powerful witness of God. From being a tomb, she's transformed into a Cathedral.

In the book of the Apocalypse 21:1–2, written in metaphoric terms is the following:

> *'Then I saw a new heaven and a new earth. The first heaven and the first earth had disappeared now, and there was no longer any sea. I saw the holy city and the new Jerusalem coming down from God out of heaven as beautiful as a bride all dressed for her husband.'*

This is what the Lord said in one of His Messages from April 3, 1995:

> *'The New Heavens ... will be when My Holy Spirit will be poured out to you all from above, from the highest Heaven ... to make a Heaven out of your soul, so that in this New Heaven I may be glorified ...*
>
> *'Let My Holy Spirit make a New Earth to prosper in your soil, so that your first earth, that was the devil's property, wears away. Then once again My Glory will shine in you and all the divine seeds sown in you by My Holy Spirit will sprout and grow in My divine Light.'*

In this Message from our Lord, 'the New Heaven and New Earth' represent metaphorically the condition of our soul. Before this renewal the soul in its sinfulness was like heaven lit by night–dark. However, with the Presence of the Holy Spirit within her, the soul now shines within and without like a thousand constellations of light, for she has received all the radiant Glory of God.

As for the New Earth, before her renewal the soul was like a wasteland, arid and dry. With the visitation of the Holy Spirit within her, she has become a New Earth, a paradise, an Eden for God, for the seeds planted in her were Divine, Celestial seeds.

The city of Jerusalem also represents our soul. We are the dwelling place of the Holy Spirit and can be called a Sanctuary, Holy Abode, Tent, City of God, Jerusalem … After this renewal, we can say that the old Jerusalem is no more; she was renewed into a new Jerusalem. In other words, her 'old self' is no more, but the new self, transformed into the light of the Holy Spirit, is now the New Jerusalem, coming out of Heaven from God. This city became God's and no longer needed the sun or the moon for light, since it was lit by the radiant Glory of God shining on her.

In this transformation the soul is now like a beautiful bride dressed for her Bridegroom, because she is dressed with Christ. The Bridegroom, who is none other than our Creator,[18] will then carry His bride into the nuptial chamber, that is to say, into His Heart.

Jesus tells us:

> *'Therefore, say to your soul, My beloved ones: "rest in God alone, for He is the only source of your hope." Let your heart exult and your soul be renewed for in these times I am pouring My graces on humanity like never before in history.'*[19]

Jesus Christ wonders why we have so much difficulty in recognizing the Signs of the Times and the sayings in Scriptures. On October 6, 1993 He asks us:

> *'Today the twigs of the fig tree are supple and its leaves are coming out; do you still not recognize the Times? How is it that so many of you cannot read and understand the Scriptures? How is it that most of you lost your perception? Have I not said: stay awake? My children, today My Kingdom is offered to you, do not pass by it without noticing it; do not let My Kingdom overtake you either; do not overlook My Love; come, I am always with you.'*

18 Isaiah 54: 5 'For now your Creator will be your husband, His Name: Yahweh Sabaoth'.

19 August 3, 2001

Many interpretations of the rapture[20] have been given, explaining that the rapture is physical. They forget that most of the time Jesus spoke either metaphorically or in parables. Concerning this issue, here are the words from Jesus that I received on July 20, 1992.

> *'Allow Me to seal your forehead with the seal of My Holy Spirit. The Time of sorting has come; the time of reckoning is here. I said to everyone that I shall come as a thief upon you. When I return no one will be suspecting anything; then, of two men one will be taken, one left; of two women one will be taken, one left.*
>
> *'The Harvest is almost ready to be reaped and countless corpses will be left when I say: "I AM here!" Then I will say to My Angel, "the hour has come to sort out and pull out all who are not Mine. Sort out from those who acknowledged Me, all those who have not willed to comply with My Law. Sort out from those who allowed and welcomed My Holy Spirit to be their Guide and their Torch, all those who rebelled in their apostasy against Me; sort out from those who are branded on the forehead with the Lamb's Seal, all those with the name of the beast or with the number 666." The Time is here and I Myself am branding My people with My Name and My Father's Name.'*

God's pedagogy – His teaching – in a way is to repeat Himself in different ways so that everyone understands His Words. The next year, on December 23, 1993, the Lord once more explained the passage above. Here are His Words:

> *'The fig tree has already formed its figs and the vines have already blossomed. Daughter, can you not see? Have you not noticed My Sign in Heaven?*[21] *Hear and write: generation, I have been sending you and I am still sending you My Angels, [messengers] to gather My chosen from the four winds – from one end of heaven to the other … Your world of today will*

20 Matthew 24: 41

21 Matthew 24: 30

wear out quickly. I am sending you My Angels to gather My elect, My people, to renew My Church. Have you not noticed? Have you not understood? Do you still not perceive My Sign?

'Today My Holy Spirit raptures one out of two, enwraps him in His blazing Fire and sends him out to be a witness to the Most High. My Holy Spirit lifts one while leaving another one behind in the dust among dust – one is taken, one left.[22] *My Holy Spirit, like the wind, blows wherever He pleases – you hear its sound but you cannot tell where it comes from or where it is going … My Holy Spirit in your days blows on you, this way and that way; His Breath is like a stream flowing in every direction and everywhere this stream flows, fruit-trees sprout up with leaves that never wither but are medicinal and everyone who eats from them is healed …*

'How is it that you cannot perceive the dazzling Light of My Holy Spirit? – Like the light of seven days in one, My Holy Spirit shines today in Heaven – is the Sign of the Son of Man appearing in Heaven not enough for you? Like a shepherd gathering his flock, My Holy Spirit gathers and saves the dispersed flock. I am revealing things hidden and unknown to you, generation, at the favorable time I am revealing you these things. Whether you turn right or left you will see this dazzling Sign in Heaven of My Holy Spirit and your ears will hear: "I AM He! I AM is with you in heart. I AM is here to build your hopes, your strength, your faith and your love."'

These passages are Spirit, and we notice that the Spirit is indeed in full action renewing God's creation. The Holy Spirit frees our spirit from sin. Flesh is flesh and so the rapture is not in flesh but in spirit. When Jesus speaks of corpses and death, it is also in spirit because sin kills us spiritually.

---

22 Again, for example, we do not know why in the same family one is lifted in the Spirit, converted and put aflame with the love of God, and not the other.

In the following Message, given on April 12, 1997, God tries to shake us up and wake up our lethargic spirit to see the Signs of the Times.

> *'The earth is in turmoil and so much innocent blood is shed; but these are also the Signs of the Times; Satan and his dark dominion are spitting out on the earth their vomit, bringing afflictions into families and divisions too; they are raising false prophets around the world producing signs and portents as well, but this is so that the elect too may fall in their treachery.'*

The world, unfortunately, is again misjudging the Times and cannot recognize them. Holy Grace is blowing upon us and in our darkness we do not notice it. God says that many of us carry war in our hearts, not peace, and this war that is carried in our hearts exteriorizes itself. Here again these words of Jesus may show a clearer vision of how our world has fallen into obscurity, and how His Hand is stretched out to help us.

On June 10, 1992, Christ said:

> *'In these Times, as never before, I reach down with My Hand from above, to save you from the powers of evil who are prepared to blow out the little light that is left in you and force you to dwell in darkness. So do not say: "there is no one to save me and no one to befriend me" and that help is denied you. Invoke Me with your heart and I will come flying to you.'*

And in another passage on September 17, 1992:

> *'I am gentle and humble of heart and I know everything in your hearts, so ask My Spirit and My Spirit will come to your help. The Spirit now asks you to pray often this prayer:*
>
> *"Jesus, neither death, nor life, no angel, no prince, nothing that exists, nothing still to come, not any power or height or depth, nor any created thing will ever come to separate me from You. I vow to remain faithful to You; this is my solemn vow; help me keep this vow forever and ever. Amen".'*

Without God in our life, there will be no peace. Without a change of heart and without love for neighbor, our world will continue to be in chaos. It's as simple as that. Without the values of life, we are heading for a major destruction caused by us and by no one else.

This is the choice that is set before you.

12

them the chance to repent; courage! I am telling you this daughter: whoever will listen let him listen; whoever will not, let him not... IXΘYΣ

20. 7. 90

O Lord, let Your Spirit rest upon me and invade me.

let Me bless you ♡ I give you My Peace; let My Spirit rest on you; I the Lord will grant you the safety you sigh for; keep firm in your faith because I am faithful to My Promise; I will put My Love Law into the hearts of your nations and I

Taken from one of Vassula's notebooks, recording a conversation with God.

13

shall never call their sins to mind; I shall remind them of My Sacrifice, I shall remind them of My Cross, I shall remind them that I am God; and you, you whom I sought and found, offer Me your heart and I shall receive it as blended incense; stay loyal to Me and yearn all that is Me to efface all that is you; annihilate all that is you by absorbing all that is Me ♡ pray for the conversion of souls, pray for peace, love and unity, remember, My Love is Infinite,

Vassula's Mission

When asked where the solution to make a better world lies, Vassula's response is "repent first, die to your ego, come back to God and pray; this is my prescription for an unhealthy and sick world".

Vassula's experiences have caused believers from all Christian denominations to raise the same question that prophets provoked in earlier times. Does Almighty God reach down to earth and speak to human beings?

The interest that Vassula's mission has created all around the world for over twenty years is a clear indication that many Christians do consider this to be the case, and that God continues to reveal Himself throughout the Christian era and into our times.

The main theme of the Messages Vassula receives continues to be the union of the Body of Christ, but at the same time her mission has reached out and been welcomed by people of all beliefs including Hindus, Moslems and Buddhists and more. Indeed many thousands from these faiths have attended her meetings and some have joined her on the True Life in God Pilgrimages. Vassula is regularly invited to attend ecumenical and interfaith conferences around the world and has been a speaker at the United Nations Headquarters in New York on *How to Obtain Peace in the Holy Land.*

Prayer Groups

God asked Vassula to form prayer groups. These are ecumenical by nature and are called True Life in God Prayer Groups and are now spread across more than 77 countries around the world, including in over 30 states across the United States.

Regional Contacts for US Prayer Groups

AA-TLIG Northeast Chapter
Email:Northeast@tlig.us

AA-TLIG Southeast Chapter
Email:southeast@tlig.us

AA-TLIG Midwest-South Chapter
Email:Midwest-South@tlig.us

AA-TLIG Midwest-North Chapter
Email:Midwest-North@tlig.us

AA-TLIG Northwest Chapter
Email:Northwest@tlig.us

AA-TLIG West Chapter
Email:West@tlig.us

Full details of prayer groups in other countries, and how to start a prayer group can be found at www.tlig.org

Pilgrimages and Retreats

Following the formation of prayer groups, Vassula was instructed to call the different Churches to pray together, to worship and have dialogues on Unity. Since then Vassula has, with the help of others, organized pilgrimages and these now take place every second year. On these pilgrimages there is a religious office each day celebrated each time by the clergy of a different Christian denomination. In Vassula's words "What is taking place in the services and meetings when all come together is so glorious because all these Churches of different denominations have already had – in an unofficial way – a foretaste of the Unity that is to come." Information about forthcoming retreats can be found at www.tlig.org

Practicing Charity

The Messages that God has given to Vassula are not only for Christians, but are for all people and it is clear that our faith must be put into action, and our love translated into the service of others.

In 1997 Vassula experienced a vision of the Virgin Mary just outside the birthplace of Christ in Bethlehem. In this vision, the Virgin Mary told her that in addition to giving people spiritual food, she needs to give people tangible food as well. In another Message, Jesus reminds Vassula "*whatever you do to the least, you do it to Me.*" With the cooperation of many volunteer workers, Vassula has now established houses –called Beth Myriams, meaning House of Mary – in 16 countries around the world. In these homes, which are open to all people regardless of faith, they offer food and care to those in need, and some provide medical care and schooling as well. Information concerning Beth Myriams can be found at www.tlig.org

True Life in God

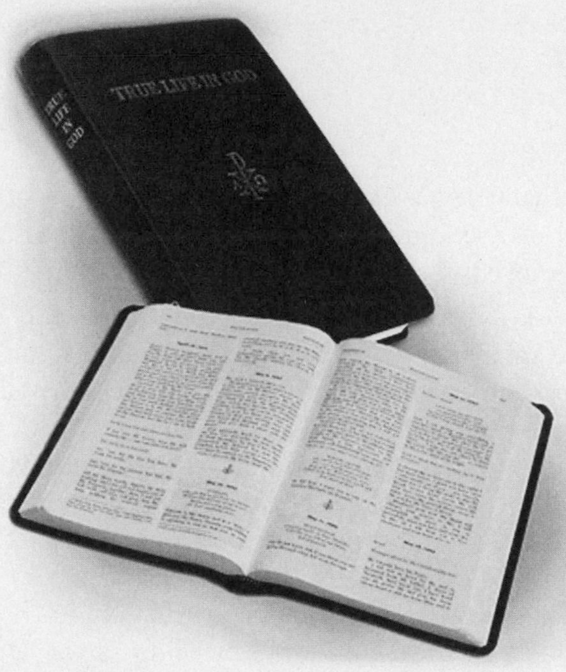

The complete True Life in God Messages are available in a single 1150 page book and in EBook format from all retailers or directly from the publisher's distributor at the following address:

National Book Network Inc
15200 NBN Way
Blue Ridge Summit
PA 17214
USA
Tel: (717) 794-3800
or 1-800-462-6420

ISBN: 978-0-9830093-1-3
Price: $39.95